FAITHFUL FRIENDS

A Jew and a Catholic Discuss Religion in Modern Life

RABBI RICHARD CHAPIN AND JEROME PITARRESI

To Connie,
a woman of faith,
a wonderful neighbor,
and a cherished friend.
With deepest affection,
Jerry
June 2014

ISBN: 1490990747
ISBN 13: 9781490990743
Library of Congress Control Number: 2013915481
CreateSpace Independent Publishing Platform,
North Charleston, South Carolina

This book is dedicated to our parents and original teachers of our faiths,
Murphy and Marjorie Pitarresi, Harold and Lila Chapin;
To our faithful companions on our life's journey, Marie and Jeanne;
To our children, the inheritors of our faith traditions,
Matthew and Marc, Joshua and Daisy.

CONTENTS

FOREWORD

This is an unusual, even astonishing book. It is a well-hewn conversation between two old friends, a Rabbi and a well-informed Catholic layman. There are no barbs or retorts or underlying tensions. Each presents his faith's position as fairly as he can and is most willing to listen to the position of the other. There are differences to be sure but there is also a wonderful unanimity of spirit. Neither says, "I am right and you are wrong."

Both agree that religion is in some difficulty today as secularism takes over our culture. Many Jews and Catholics alike are, if not officially leaving their respective traditions, simply no longer taking an active part. Family life has become frayed; desire for "things" has become rampant. Religion as a social glue to hold communities and families together has become less and less successful.

Secular Democratic-Capitalism sounds great, particularly when the idea that all people are "created equal" is stressed, but, in fact, there are many other social values that it is difficult to come by through secularism. Rabbi Richard Chapin and Jerome Pitarresi reveal in their conversations how important family values, forgiveness, compassion, and many other Judeo-Christian virtues really are both for individuals and for society.

Today, although secularism seems to grow stronger every day, our consciences are still informed, at least in part, by the Hebrew Scriptures and the New Testament. If that influence were to disappear, it is difficult to know how society would define its essential values. The authors of this work reveal how important basic values from the Bible still inform them and provide a basis for action.

So I recommend this book most highly for anyone concerned about where America and the world are headed. It presents religion from the inside, as a way of life that provides meaning and purpose for existence. It reveals why many still cling to the ancient traditions that have so defined Western society. Its importance may indeed be greater than even the authors realize.

Jay G. Williams
Walcott-Bartlett Professor of Religious Studies, emeritus
Hamilton College

INTRODUCTION: WE BEGIN WITH A PUN!

RICHARD CHAPIN (RC) TO JEROME PITARRESI (JP)

I haven't forgotten our project. I'm reading an article in the *New Yorker* about a new biography of James Joyce by Louis Menand. As you know, Joyce was a terrific punster. He once said to a friend, "After all, the Holy Roman Catholic Apostolic Church was built on a pun. It ought to be good enough for me." Joyce meant the verse in Matthew 16:18 in which Jesus tells Simon Peter, "You are Peter, and on this rock I will build my church." The pun, of course, is on the Anglicization of the Greek *petros*.

I like Menand's description of a pun. He calls it a "verbal coincidence—a word that just happens to sound like another word. In this respect, the whole of Joyce's *Ulysses* is a kind of pun. It's a story about people and events on a day in Dublin that, when told in a certain way, sounds like Homer's *Odyssey*."

And this may be a good place to start our "conversations." Joyce certainly had a lot of trouble with the Church. In *Ulysses*, he won't even pray with his mother on her deathbed! But my question, and of course you are free to go any direction you like in your response, is this: How and on what grounds do we build our faith?

The rock is a great place to start, and Peter, well, he is intriguing…to say the least. He may be compared to the Israelites, who, having witnessed God's miracles in the desert, still deny him in their moments of anxiety (which were more than moments—they were constant). In Matthew 16:18–19, Peter is assured by the Savior that the Church will be built "on" him and that he will receive the keys of the kingdom of heaven, yet when pressed near the end, he *still* denies Jesus three times (Matt. 26:69–75). Oh, ye of little faith….

At any rate, I thought we could start some point-counterpoint, perhaps not too systematically at the moment. But let's get started and see where we go from here.

All good things, dear friend.

JERRY PITARRESI (JP) TO RICHARD CHAPIN (RC)

To say that I'm excited about the prospect of doing something literary with you is an understatement—I'm elated. And to begin our "conversations" with the famous play on words (names and words, really) attributed to Jesus in entrusting his nascent church to Peter's leadership is appropriate. Jesus knew Peter better than Peter knew himself. How and on what faith is built are two very intriguing questions. Peter built his faith on Jesus. In response to Jesus's question, "But who do *you* say I am?" Peter asserts, "You are the Messiah, the son of the Living God" (Matt. 16:15-16). Peter steadfastly accompanied Jesus during his three-year ministry and witnessed his miracles and transfiguration (where he heard God the Father say that Jesus was his beloved son). Tragically, Peter wavered—no, crumbled—when Jesus needed him most. He wasn't the only one to fail Jesus, but he was most notable because of his protestations that he would never deny his Lord and Savior. By the time the cock crowed, Peter had done just that, three times.

Oh, ye of little faith, indeed. The Rock didn't seem to warrant the confidence Jesus had in him. In fact, he seemed more sand than rock—not a good foundation on which to build a church. But of course, that's not the end of the story for Peter or for the church that Jesus entrusted to his leadership. Redemption is possible; it turns out that Jesus's faith in Peter to be his Rock was not misplaced after all. I see the parallel with the Israelites and the God they turned away from despite all he had done to show his love for them. Ultimately, they are reconciled, and the covenant is restored between Yahweh and his Chosen People.

I'll ruminate on the questions you've posed, Richard. They're interesting ones, and I'll do my best to answer them. Perhaps our long, deep friendship helps to provide an answer—faith, like friendship, is built on beliefs, values, and experiences. Faith is an individual matter, but I think it's strengthened through communal gatherings and rituals.

RC Well, you've got me hauling out scholarly volumes on the New Testament…the Synoptic Gospel Parallels—the Gospels of Mark, Matthew, and Luke—"seen together." Perhaps the most scholarly work I have in my library is *The Death of the Messiah*, a two-volume study by Raymond E. Brown. What a scholar! As a Roman Catholic priest, the first Roman Catholic professor at Union Theological for nearly three decades, Brown was often criticized for employing the historical-critical method in his scholarship.

Let's stay on the subject of Peter, first known as Simon, who later becomes the "rock," (in Aramaic, *cephas*). And yet, as you pointed out in your first epistle, "sand" may have been a more appropriate image for him in his threefold denial of Jesus.

Yet it is all predicted by Jesus—including, of course, Judas's betrayal of his Master to the chief priests for money. So here we are in the midst of the Passion Narrative, which of course is the crux (pun intended) of the New Testament narrative, and everything seems to be falling apart…or is it?

I think of the Exodus narrative and the ten plagues the Almighty inflicted upon our Egyptian adversaries. Why did he do it? Clearly, God could have freed the Israelites at any time with one stroke of his awesome power. Yet he prolonged the story by "hardening the Pharaoh's heart" after each plague. Why? To teach the Israelites, step by step, to accept and believe in his mighty acts. And they do finally believe, after seeing the death of the firstborns in all Egypt, human and animal, that God, and concomitantly they, are victorious. Yet throughout the desert wanderings, they return constantly to the state of "disbelief," and they constantly need to be buoyed up by the miracles God performs and the admonitions of Moses.

So I'm wondering…is there a parallel here in the New Testament relationship between Jesus and his disciples, and particularly between Jesus and Peter? Jesus's disciples, although they follow and witness the miracles of their Master, are slow to recognize his divinity (particularly in the gospel of Mark). And even when they do, they are quick to disavow their Master, either through Judas's sin of greed, or through Peter's fear of being associated with Jesus, which may be viewed as a lack of faith.

In other words, is Jesus teaching, through the Passion narrative, that redemption and faith in the World to Come must be acquired through failure to believe in those two intertwined subjects? It is not until Peter fails to acknowledge the Savior three separate times (and the cock's "calling" him on that egregious sin) that he "gets it." Because it is Peter/Simon who is first approached by Jesus after the resurrection. Peter, who does not possess the strength of his faith, who had "wept bitterly" after denying his relationship with Jesus, finally sees Jesus for who he truly is: "The Lord has risen indeed, and he has appeared to Simon!" (Lk 24:34).

We like to trot out the old saw *seeing is believing*. Yet the Israelites saw, the disciples saw—and they still wavered in their faith in the Lord. Is that man's fate? Drawn to the material world of money and flesh, we are forever skeptical about the world of the spirit. Therefore we stumble, fall, get up, and do it again (and again) until we see the light. Jesus seemed to understand this; so did Moses. People fall down constantly in their attempts to ascend the altar of faith and conviction. They need to be constantly inspired by the lessons of our faiths.

And who, having read the Bible and the New Testament, ever thought it would be easy?

JP Your knowledge and understanding of the Gospels is more thorough than that of some Christians I know—many, actually. That doesn't surprise me, of course. Jesus, as the "new Moses," did have problems when it came to the intimate little band he led—Moses just had a ton more "stiff-necked" people to keep in line. Of course, it's easy to have faith in God when everything is going fine, but it's quite another thing to maintain that belief when adversity strikes. There aren't many Jobs among us. Plus the answer that Job gets when he finally cries out to God doesn't satisfy many people: God's ways are not man's way; we humans cannot plumb the mind of the Almighty. Human beings are always seeking answers to mysteries—e.g., the recent discovery of the Higgs Boson, or "God particle," as physicists have dubbed it. Taking on faith something that can't be seen is a leap that many people can't or won't make.

I've always liked the following quotation from Pierre Teilhard de Chardin regarding faith and our human nature: "We are not human beings having a spiritual experience; we are spiritual beings having a human experience." In terms of faith, I think our spiritual development often progresses like other parts of our life. We learn to walk first by crawling, then by toddling. So it is with faith, though I would not discount that a conversion experience like Saul/Paul's—who gets the message directly *from* Jesus when he's struck by a blinding light on the road to Damascus—is possible. Born-again Christians certainly believe that. I'm a bit skeptical about some "instant" faith conversions, but I won't dismiss the idea that all things are possible with God.

Regarding your question about Jesus's intent with his disciples and their belief in him, I'm not sure that he necessarily ordained that their road to belief had to have so many stumbling blocks, but he certainly knew that that path would be difficult for even the closest and most loyal of his followers, even Peter, the "rock" in whom he put the most trust. He told them repeatedly that following him would exact a great cost, in many cases, their lives. The payoff, if you want to call it that, would be the ushering in of the Kingdom of God on earth and eternal life with God in Heaven. That leap of faith was something the apostles have difficulty with when Jesus suffers his Passion—he knows he must go through the humiliation of arrest, the mock trial, the scourging, and the crucifixion to redeem them and the rest of humanity, but they look upon his ministry as a failed endeavor—until, of course, the resurrection three days after his death.

What I find interesting, as well as ironic, in the depiction of faith in the New Testament, is how people who weren't in Jesus's "inner circle," complete strangers really, showed the deepest faith in his ability to cure them or someone they loved. Jairus, a synagogue official, and the woman who suffered from hemorrhages (Mk 5:21–43), as well as the Roman centurion who asked Jesus to heal his paralyzed servant (Matt. 8:5–13) are examples that come to mind. Why were these people able to place such complete trust in Jesus while his own disciples wavered in theirs? Peter, for example, is depicted as being afraid when Jesus calls to him to walk on the water while they are on the Sea of Galilee in one scene from the Gospels (Matt. 14:22–33), a foreshadowing, perhaps, of his failure of faith and loyalty in the more crucial scene of Jesus's Passion.

The disciples sank to the nadir of their faith after the crucifixion. Their Master, the one they believed to be the Messiah, had suffered and died the most ignoble of deaths. He was gone from their midst, and they were a dispirited band. But just as God hadn't abandoned the Israelites in their travails in exile in Egypt and on their journey through the desert, Jesus hadn't left his followers completely bereft. He did appear to them in several post-resurrection episodes to prove to them that he was who he said he was, the Son of God. Before he went to his Father, he promised that he would send the Paraclete, the Holy Spirit, to strengthen them in their faith. That gift was bestowed on the disciples at Pentecost, and it infused them with renewed belief in Jesus and in the Gospel message of salvation, which they began to preach to people of all backgrounds. In a scene that could be seen as the negative image of the Tower of Babel, the apostles address people who speak many different languages, and each understands them.

The point here is that faith is a gift of God that people are free to embrace or not to embrace. As you said, Jesus knew that "the spirit is willing, but the flesh is weak," that human beings are subject to doubts and temptations, which can cause them to stumble on their spiritual journey. The Israelites had Moses and the prophets, gifts from God really, to guide them on their spiritual paths. At times they strayed, despite the guidance and exhortations of Moses and the prophets. Jesus, the "new Moses," can also be seen as a gift of God to the people of his time (and our time as well, of course). Many people listened to his message, but others ultimately rejected it. In Jesus's physical absence, the gift of the Holy Spirit serves to connect Christians with the truth of his message of a right relationship with God and their fellow human beings, and ultimately, of the path to eternal salvation. People sometimes turn away from that message and wander from the path, more so today, it seems, with the "attractions" of the material, fleshly world calling out so loudly. Apostasy is clearly part of the human condition and perhaps when the apostate finds his or her way back to God, the commitment he or she makes to a life of faith is stronger and more enduring.

At present, the world of the flesh speaks more loudly and convincingly to many people than does the world of the spirit. Like the Israelites, we have our false gods and a prideful nature that places God on the periphery rather than at the center of our lives. But the story is not over.

QUESTIONS OF FAITH

Have you not known? Have you not heard? The LORD is the everlasting God, the Creator of the ends of the earth. He does not faint or grow weary; his understanding is unsearchable. He gives power to the faint, and strengthens the powerless. Even youths will faint and be weary, and the young will fall exhausted; but those who wait for the LORD shall renew their strength, they shall mount up with wings like eagles, they shall run and not be weary, they shall walk and not faint (Isa. 40:28–31).

RC Faith. Why do we believe? Why are many of us fervent about our faith? Why, on the other hand, have so many abandoned their faith and developed disdain for it?

Why do we believe? A very good question, coupled with its opposite—why is it that many people today either *don't* believe or don't feel a strong attraction to their faith, in whatever tradition they were raised?

For most of us, faith is part of our heritage. That is, our parents, who believed in their respective traditions, made sure that we, their offspring, were brought up to believe in Catholicism and Judaism as part of our religious inheritance. Many of us still carry with us those early religious experiences, both at home and in the sanctuary, but there comes a point at which we must decide how we are going to internalize those beliefs and practices into our own lives, and hopefully transmit them to our own children as well. The responsibility for our children's observance lies with every generation of parents. And yet, clearly the transmission is not always successful, to be sure.

JP As Catholic parents, Marie and I made sure our sons attended Sunday Mass with us, went to religious education classes, and made their First Communions and their Confirmations. We were involved in our parish as lectors; we read to them from books on the saints; and we said the rosary as a family—family trips in the car usually began with its recitation. Somehow, though, we either failed to communicate how important our faith is to us, or they have chosen to place the beliefs they grew up with in the back of their minds. The world speaks too loudly to them at the moment, perhaps; the voice of faith has been muted. Still, we have to believe that it remains part of who they are.

RC *Failure* is a strong word, Jerry. It is not unusual for young people to become less observant, particularly when they leave home for college. I prefer to think of your boys, Matt and Marc, as having entered a period that might appropriately be called *dormant*. As you like to say, Marie and you have spent a lot of time "sowing the seeds" of faith in your sons. You cannot compel the boys to practice their faith, but you've done everything possible, in my view, to convince them of the value of preserving Catholicism in their homes and in their lives.

JP I guess our responsibility as parents is to show our children the path of faith; we can't compel them to take the steps on that journey if they are not so inclined. Speaking of spirituality, I tell the students in my religious education class that we are all at different places on the journey of faith; some are farther down the path than others. I have to remember that as I think about my own sons in terms of their faith—and trust in God that the seed that was planted will continue to grow.

RC I feel that way about my son, Josh, who is a contemporary of your boys. I'm less worried about his observance than his commitment to preserve his Jewish heritage. How that manifests is another thing. He doesn't have to believe and practice like his father. He doesn't have to be a Hebraist, and he certainly doesn't have to be a rabbi (although ironically, I thought he had all the requisite rabbinical "markings"). It's bad enough that he became a Bills fan like his dad, despite the fact that he grew up in New York City! But I'm not worried if he doesn't go to temple on Friday night or Saturday morning. He is Jewish by birth, but he also chooses to be Jewish in his daily life. In fact, he's in Israel for the first time as we speak, on the Birthright program. I was always careful, particularly considering my vocation, not to demand too much of him in terms of active observance of his faith.

JP Perhaps the best approach is not to demand that our sons follow our path of faith, but rather to allow them to find it for themselves, with our guidance, of course. That itself requires faith on our part that what we have done to instruct our children in the realm of spirituality will bear fruit.

RC Yes, *faith* is derived from the Latin word *fides*, which means "trust" or "confidence." We have to be confident that the way we have lived our lives and observed our faiths will continue through our children's belief and practice. It's not, as people like to say, a crapshoot. Faith is a continuous process and a continuous goal. We all have doubts, even the most orthodox observers, about how we should believe. But when I see parents passing the Torah to their children on the day of their bar or bat mitzvah, I know they understand the mission—it's too literal a moment to miss! When we return the Torah to the ark, we recite the words: "Behold, a good doctrine has been given unto you; forsake it not." That's our obligation; we pray that our children will see that it is *their* obligation too.

JP Confidence means putting faith in not just what we have taught our children, but also in what we believe God's plan is for them.

RC So God will watch over your children. This I believe. In this plan, I remain confident for both our families. May it be true for all of us who wish the same for our beloved offspring.

WHERE IT ALL BEGAN: JEWISH AND CHRISTIAN LESSONS

JEWISH LESSONS

A five-year-old begins Scripture; a ten-year-old begins Mishnah, the study of the Law... (Sayings of the Fathers 5:25).

RC Well, we've already covered some interesting ground. Questions raised by our respective testaments have brought about other questions. This is as it should be. Judaism's greatest philosopher of the twentieth century, Abraham Joshua Heschel, said: "We must pray to God not for the answers to our problems but rather for the strength to ask the right questions." That has always been the Jewish way. We have been a people who, from the very beginning of the biblical narrative, were loathe to accept superficial answers to our questions. While we consider the Bible our greatest book (the translation of the Greek *ho biblos* is "the book"), it only initiates our studies. Listen to what it says in a tractate of the Mishnah (a commentary on the biblical laws) known as the *Pirkei Avot,* (Sayings of the Fathers) (5:25):

"A five-year-old begins Scripture; a ten-year-old begins Mishnah, a study of the Law; a fifteen-year-old begins to study Talmud."

It's an impressive *curriculum*. That is a word I've always employed in my rabbinic teaching. A curriculum, as you well know as a lifelong teacher, is something that must be followed and attended to on a regular basis. I believe that is Judaism's greatest strength. The acquisition of knowledge begins as a scholastic endeavor, but it is a process that occupies us throughout our allotment of days on this precious earth. Knowledge, discussion, commentary, and legal and narrative perplexities—all of these are primary pursuits for those who wish to lead enriched Jewish existences.

So let's lay our scholastic cards on the table, Monsieur Pitarresi. I remember my friends in elementary school (Herbert Hoover in Kenmore, New York) leaving school early one day a week for RI—religious instruction. I assume you were among that saintly number. What did you study? We had pre–bar/bat mitzvah preparation. After the age of thirteen, most of us elected to continue our religious "studies" (that term may be euphemistic) for our confirmation ceremony, which took place in tenth grade. A very few of us continued to attend a Jewish high school through our twelfth grade religious school graduation.

For most liberal Jews, this was the end of any formal Jewish education. Unless students enrolled for Judaic courses at college or university (we never had the opportunity at Hamilton in the late ‘60s), our respective RIs were over. I know adult education courses proliferate at most synagogues and churches, but the subjects offered are usually short-term, and they are often based on what rabbis and ministers think their congregants will enjoy rather than what is academically substantive.

I’ve often said that Reform Judaism was a great course of study for rabbis. We immerse ourselves in traditional sources, parse them, and then distill them for our communities, who neither have the religious nor linguistic background to approach them on more than a beginner-to-intermediate level. How have you done it, Jerry? How did you acquire, and how have you continued to acquire, knowledge of your Christian faith and religion?

CHRISTIAN LESSONS: CATECHISM

Parents have the first responsibility for the education of their children. They bear witness to this responsibility by creating a home where tenderness, forgiveness, fidelity, and disinterested service are the rule. The home is well suited for education in the virtues (The Catechism of the Catholic Church #2223).

JP Your recollection of your Catholic classmates at Herbert Hoover Elementary in Kenmore leaving school early for religious instruction took me back more than fifty years. As members of the Diocese of Buffalo as well, we kids in Niagara Falls trekked off, *religiously,* you might say, to our parish school once a week to learn about our Catholic faith. Our parents took seriously their responsibility to raise us in the faith. As young Catholics, we either went to parochial school, or we went to religious instruction—all of my Catholic friends did one or the other. I don't recall anyone "opting out."

The classes were taught by a faculty of nuns, seminarians, and laypeople. The text we studied from was called the *Baltimore Catechism*; almost all Catholic Baby Boomers would be familiar with that tome. Because religious figures (nuns, priests, brothers) were more abundant in those days, laypeople were in the minority; today, of course, the landscape has changed dramatically, and most religious education classes are taught by laypeople, in some cases, even students in junior high. The efficacy of such a situation is, predictably, not optimal, but it is the reality the Church is facing at this juncture in its history.

Catholic schools were much more prevalent during the Baby Boom than they are today, and we had the opportunity to attend our parish school instead of the public schools in Niagara Falls. Education in one's Catholic faith wasn't limited to one hour a week at Prince of Peace School—the curriculum often included daily Mass and instruction in the faith. For whatever reason, except for my brother John, who spent one year at the Catholic high school, none of our brood of ten attended parochial school. Still, our parents made sure we went to religious instruction each week, along with attending Mass each Sunday. In our parish, the 9:15 a.m. service was a children's Mass. Our pastor, Monsignor Carey, presided, and his homily was directed at the young people in the congregation. We sat dutifully in the first pews of the church, right in front of the pulpit. A nun sat at the end of each pew to make sure we paid attention to Monsignor Carey's homily. So I guess you could say that we had *two* hours of religious instruction each week, because we were definitely being schooled in our faith on Sunday as well.

A word about our home life seems in order here as I contemplate your query about how I acquired knowledge of my Christian, specifically Catholic, faith. It has been said that a child's first teachers (and perhaps most important ones) are his or her parents, and in terms of my acquisition of faith, I can attest to the validity of that statement. My parents were devout Catholics—my mother had gone to Catholic schools for her entire education, and she worked as a nurse in a Catholic hospital. My father attended Niagara University, an institution run by the Vincentian Fathers, where courses in theology were a mandatory part of the curriculum. As I mentioned, we attended Mass each Sunday, and we recited the rosary frequently as a family. Religious pictures hung from our walls, and Bishop Fulton J. Sheen, an erudite theologian and gifted speaker, was a weekly visitor to our home, courtesy of the new medium of television. My mother subscribed to a Catholic book club for us children, and my father had a bookshelf filled with more weighty books on the Catholic faith, St. Augustine's *Confessions,* and the writings of Saint Thomas Aquinas, for example, complemented by magazines such as *St. Anthony Messenger* and *America* (the latter is published by the Society of Jesus, the Jesuits). Thanks to our parents, committed to passing their strong religious beliefs on to their children, we were very conscious of our faith and thought of it as part of our identity, both as individuals and as a family.

The nuns we had for religious instruction, it seemed, believed that they had to drill quite a bit of theology into us because they had us for only one hour a week. They force-fed us from *The Baltimore Catechism.* The one part of that book most of us Baby Boomer Catholics can recite from memory is the following:

> Question: Why did God make us?
>
> Answer: God made us to know, love, and serve him in this world, and to be happy with him in the next.

That concept was easy enough to grasp, but as the years went by, the theology became a bit more difficult to plumb. The concepts of the Trinity, for instance—the Father, Son, and Holy Spirit, three distinct parts of the Godhead, but yet one—and transubstantiation, the miraculous process by which ordinary bread and wine truly become the body and blood of Jesus Christ during the Eucharistic offering of the Mass.

For most Catholics, preparation for two important sacraments, First Communion and Confirmation, comprises the means by which they gain knowledge of their faith. First Communion takes place when a child is in second grade; Catholics are usually confirmed at the age of fifteen or sixteen. Once a bishop has confirmed a young Catholic, that individual is considered an adult in the eyes of the Church. And for many of them, that represents the end of any search for and acquisition of knowledge of their faith (and, in many cases, active participation in that faith, especially in today's culture).

Personally, I have found several ways to continue learning about my faith as an adult. Books and magazines are both helpful resources I use to further my knowledge of Catholic theology and teachings. Parish retreats focused on a spiritual theme are another opportunity I have embraced to deepen my understanding of my faith. I've also been to larger, diocesan-wide retreats, one specifically for men (with more than one thousand men in attendance). Beyond those vehicles for gaining more knowledge of my faith, I make it a practice to read the Scripture passages for daily Mass, along with meditations on them. While the readings are weighted more heavily toward the New Testament, passages from the Old Testament appear as well. And of course, the Internet offers no lack of websites that offer information and inspiration to anyone who seeks to learn more about his or her own religion. My caveat is that such sites need to be chosen judiciously; I often use the website of the United States Conference of Catholic Bishops (usccb.org) to delve into subjects of faith I want to know more about.

So I would say the path toward acquiring knowledge of one's faith is not so very different for a young Catholic and for his or her Jewish counterpart. The formal religious education of both seems to end at about the same time. Additional insights into Catholicism are available to those who attend Catholic high schools and colleges, or who feel compelled by some inner voice (the Holy Spirit?) to seek more knowledge on their own. What happens after a Catholic's formal education in his or her faith is complete can differ greatly from person to person.

COPING WITH TRAGEDY

Comfort, o comfort my people, says your God. (Isa. 40:1)

Come to me, all you that are weary and are carrying heavy burdened, and I will give you rest (Matt. 11:28).

RC You have spoken of a recent tragedy in your hometown. Can we take some time to talk about it?

JP The tragedy involves a 2012 graduate of our high school here in central New York, who had just entered her freshman year in college. She was brutally murdered in her dorm room, and her boyfriend, also from our town, has been charged with her death. The shock waves continue to reverberate through our whole community.

RC That's as bad as it gets. It's one thing to lose a loved one who has lived a "full" life. It's another to lose a child who is just beginning hers. And to lose someone in such a violent way. How is the family coping with this senseless act?

JP They attend our church, and I saw them at Mass last Sunday. Perhaps I was reading into their body language and expressions too much, but they appeared as grief-stricken as one might imagine—they wore somber, numb expressions whenever I glanced in their direction. Actually, I was surprised to see them in church a week after their daughter's horrible death. It's clear that they are drawing strength from the outpouring of support and sympathy from everyone in New Hartford and the entire area. Today's paper has an article headlined "Family Begins 'Purple Pinkie' Campaign in Victim's Memory." They are determined to keep their daughter's memory alive in a positive way—purple was her favorite color and has been chosen as the color for October's Domestic Violence Awareness Campaign. Most of the trees in our village have purple ribbons wrapped around their trunks. From something so negative, the family is reaching for something positive. Not all parents could find the strength to do that. I'm not sure I could.

RC Yes, it is remarkable what they're doing. Over the years, during my rabbinate, I have seen exactly the opposite behavior prevail in families' darkest hours. I'm very inspired by that family's remarkable strength. That they are turning to the community and to the church, the emblem of community, speaks volumes about their commitment to God and humanity. And I don't want to label this turning as *catharsis*. I find it very sad that those who do not observe their religion at church or synagogue cannot really understand or begin to appreciate what solace a religious community can bring to those who are suffering. Clearly, and I learned this very early in my clerical career, many people sit in pews each weekend who have experienced difficulties in their life. The consolation those hours spent in the company of like-minded parishioners cannot be measured materially. But it is essential to their survival.

JP The whole community has reached out and embraced the family, which has been deeply touched. Two families, really, have been devastated by this unspeakable event, and it has served to make us a bit more appreciative of the goodness people can demonstrate, even as we see how violence and the dark side of human nature is not far removed from our own midst. The young people of our community, those who knew the victim as well as those who didn't, have been greatly affected, as one might expect. At the same time, the adults here, especially those who are parents, have also been rocked by the tragedy. Did we somehow fail this young man who grew up in our schools and on our playing fields? We have to face the unthinkable and search for answers where none may be found. It has definitely been a communal sharing of grief and questioning.

RC When we witness all the tragedies in the world, but particularly in America—I surely don't have to recount them here—we tend to try to answer the question of why. That is, why could someone kill people in a theater or in a school, or in this case, in a dorm room? What was the motivation? And could it have been prevented? Frankly, I'm angered by the TV programs, newspaper and Internet accounts, and blogs that "search" for the right answers.

The Bible and the New Testament uphold the Ten Commandments as the basis for human behavior. Clearly the act of murder is unmistakably in that number: "Thou shalt not murder." Whatever happened to this young man—you've indicated that he might have been on steroids at the time—does not excuse his sinful act. It is a sin to take a life unless you are preventing someone from harming your family or your person. I remember Oscar Hijuelos's book, *Mr. Ives' Christmas*, in which a man whose son was murdered spends the rest of the narrative trying to forgive the murderer. It does help him.

But if it helped him, it certainly doesn't help those of us who are sickened by the violence so prevalent in society. It used to be that when your girlfriend broke up with you, you wrote a letter and told her how much you missed her. Or you called her. This recent act is unforgivable by law and by religion. Unfortunately, Jerry, this "searching for answers" keeps repeating itself in every community that experiences these senseless acts. Are parents at fault for these tragedies? Is society? I think the questions are easier than the answers, and I refer once again to Abraham Joshua Heschel, who said: "We pray to God not for the answers but for the strength to ask the right questions."

JP To take another life, under any circumstances other than self-defense or defense of one's loved ones, I agree, is a violation of both God's law and that of humankind. Who is at fault? "It takes a village to raise a child," the proverb states. Is the *village* responsible for what that child becomes—in this case, a murderer? Does the responsibility stop at the front door of the house where the young man, the assailant, lived? Perhaps all of us in our town have been so deeply affected by this tragedy not only because a bright young woman's promising life was taken from her so prematurely but also because we feel some sense of culpability that the young man who ended it so violently grew up in our midst.

RC Yes, there is a collective guilt. We just finished the Holy Days. We say a lot of prayers confessing our sins—Yom Kippur is an entire liturgy of listing our failings. And perhaps there is a feeling, as a community, that by the end of the day, we have "earned" God's forgiveness for another year (we refer to it as being written into the Book of Life) by sincere repentance. But in this case, I'm reminded of the line Robin Williams kept saying to Matt Damon in *Good Will Hunting*: "It's not your fault; it's not your fault; it's not your fault...." until Matt Damon broke down in his arms.

It's not your community's fault, Jerry. It is the fault of this young man. I guess he'll have a lot of time to repent and seek forgiveness in his jail cell, but I don't feel sympathy for him, and neither should the community. His family? Well, that's another matter entirely. They will suffer the rest of their lives for this murderous act of their son. That is a sentence they don't deserve, but it is a sentence they'll have to live with, whether they choose to participate in the community or not in the future.

SPIRITUALITY

By contrast the fruit of the Spirit is love, joy, peace, patience, kindness, generosity, faithfulness, gentleness, and self-control... (Gal. 5:22–23).

RC A story. . .which leads to a discussion about spirituality. Years ago, at Temple Emanu-El of New York, I performed the bat mitzvah ceremony for a thirteen-year-old named Bevin Kaplan. Twenty-two years later she called me and asked if I would perform the wedding ceremony for her and her fiancé, Danny. It was a destination wedding in La Jolla, California.

Why would she call me after so many years? I knew there was something more than the fact that I was the rabbi who had officiated at her bat mitzvah. I wasn't sure what it was, but I hoped I would learn more when we met. During the weekend, prior to the wedding, Bevin introduced me to a lifelong girlfriend who wanted to read an excerpt from the children's story *The Runaway Bunny* during the ceremony. Well, I was nonplussed, Jerry. Was this an appropriate reading for a wedding ceremony? I Googled the story, which tells about a mother trying to reassure her child that wherever the child is, she will be there with her. It's charming, and as you now remind me, this is the same author who wrote the more famous *Goodnight Moon,* Margaret Wise Brown. (Thank you, Jerry.) At any rate, Google referred me to Psalm 139:7–8 "Where can I go from thy spirit? Or where can I flee from your presence? If I ascend to heaven, you are there: if I make my bed in Sheol, you are there." And this is where Bevin and I connected. We believe that God, a protective, redeeming God, is with us wherever we are. It's something Bevin and I agreed upon minutes before the ceremony took place! I always feel privileged when asked to perform a wedding ceremony. But this special insight afforded me by Bevin will always make this one of the most memorable of my seventeen hundred nuptial celebrations!

JP Having read *The Runaway Bunny* many times to our boys at bedtime, I'm familiar with the book. At the time I saw it as a story that reassured the boys that their mom and I would always be there for them—and now, more than twenty years later, I see the truth of that. Reading Psalm 139 just now, I can see that God, in his all-seeing, all-knowing, all-present nature, stands in the same relationship to us as the mother rabbit does to her little bunny. He knows each of us, his creations—better, perhaps, than we know ourselves. I'm not sure I really understood or appreciated that truth when I was Bevin's age. The spiritual journey is a very personal and individual one.

One of my friends, a lapsed Catholic (sadly, one of many I know) told me this morning that he had no belief in an afterlife. The Bible, in his mind, was a worthy book, because it presented people with a moral code, with rules to live by, but he felt that religion has done more to divide and inflict suffering on people than it has to unite and uplift them. He didn't believe that worshipping in a building was essential to leading a spiritual life. That feeling seems to be a popular one these days.

RC Yes, I've had my problems with the term *spirituality* over the years. As you suggest, the addition of other forms of so-called spiritual expression—be it yoga, meditation, or a dash of Buddhism here and there—have sufficed for many who choose to lead completely secular lives. I find this development sad and, at worst, tragic. There is nothing wrong with supplementing one's religion with these so-called spiritual exercises. But one should be careful not to make those supplements to our religion the religion itself!

JP Your phrase *supplements to our religion* made me think of other activities that have the power to move and affect people. Sports come to mind. I played sports in high school and college, and I ran for many years after college. Though I derived many benefits from my athletic endeavors, I don't think they took on a deeper significance for me—certainly not a spiritual one. They helped me understand my physical self, my body, and its abilities and its limits, but they didn't have any effect on my spirituality, except perhaps to be thankful that God gave me the gift of health, which enabled me to enjoy sports.

RC Exactly. You can develop a "need" to exercise on a daily basis. You can derive satisfaction from a good round of golf. But do these relate to the concept of spirituality? When I hear people speak at funerals about how much their father loved golf, I get depressed. I understand the golf "fraternity," and I know how painful it is to lose someone in the foursome because of death. But we used to call exercise "fun," or a "pleasant diversion," and that was it. I think the problem goes back to the understanding of *religion,* which is a word that means "binding." Perhaps that is it, Jerry. Very few of us want to be bound or beholden to an idea that requires a regular commitment, i.e., church or synagogue. We don't want to be lectured to or harangued by, God forbid, our minister or rabbi, about what we "should" be doing in our lives. We want control of our own destinies. The idea that we should submit to anyone else—or anyone Else—is anathema, somehow endangering our freedom of "entitlement," perhaps the preeminent word of the individual living in twenty-first-century America. Religion, as you know, is submission to God, a recognition that there is something much greater than us, and that idea is what we pay homage to. God is immanent. He exists, and our prayers pay homage to the truth of his eternal existence. That is what the Psalm asserts: God is here, there, and everywhere. The message is "Pray for all you're worth and thus earn His blessing."

JP *Commitment* is a key word. Perhaps my being married for thirty-eight years to the same woman speaks to my feelings about that idea. But we do seem to see less willingness on the part of people to commit to things—service organizations, for example, have a difficult time enlisting new members. Our parish has a staff that is older—the pastor is the youngest person, and he is in his late fifties. Our music director is in her mid-eighties. I don't see people standing in line to take over these positions. Maybe it's because people are too busy—most families have both husband and wife working. I see grandparents picking up children from preschool at our church. But I think you touched on a vital issue when you mentioned the word *entitlement.* People want what they want, and they don't want to think that, for whatever reason, they are not in control of their own lives. Religion just doesn't have a very high priority in their lives—at least not until some tragedy occurs or they want to get married or buried. The point of religion is that we have a relationship with God, and that, by definition, is something that necessitates maintaining a dialogue and a connection, through prayer, both personal and communal. That sounds old fashioned by today's mores, doesn't it?

RC We're "hopelessly" old-fashioned, to be sure, but thankfully, dear friend, we still possess hope in our hearts and in our souls. It is a religious hope that God constantly watches over us and those we love.

Let's pray for our new bride and groom, Bevin and Danny, **(and their newborn child!)** and hope that God will continue to bestow his hand of blessing upon them, today and all days.

JP I join you in that prayer for Bevin and Danny and their newly arrived gift from God. In the past four months, Marie and I have attended six weddings; a seventh will take place at the end of December. We have a little custom of holding hands at the vows, praying for the new couple as they make their pledge of mutual fidelity while at the same time renewing our own commitment to one another. We feel God has blessed our marriage, and we wish for that same blessing to fall upon the young couple.

RC Amen. May it be so. Until next time, dear friend.

SEX

Sexual union should be consummated only out of desire and as a result of joy of the husband and wife.

—Maimonides

RC We turn now, Jerry, to a subject for the ages. *Sex*. Everyone has opinions about it, everyone wants to hear about it, and everyone seems unsure what their respective religion says about it. According to Rabbi Hayim Levy Donin in his essential guide to Jewish life, "To Be A Jew":

> While Judaism condemns any kind of "forbidden" sexuality (sodomy, adultery, promiscuity, harlotry, etc.), it speaks with glowing enthusiasm for the beauty of the sexual relationship when expressed in the intimate love between a man and a woman within the sanctified union of marriage.

And here's the clincher: "The beauty, the character and even the health of the offspring were thought by our Sages to be influenced by the quality of the sexual relationship."

JP Sex and the Catholic Church is a topic that could engender some heated discussion, to be sure. The Church doesn't pretend that sex doesn't exist; rather, it acknowledges that "male and female He [God] created them" and gave Adam and Eve the command to "be fruitful and multiply." Love is a gift of God, meant to be shared. Human sexuality is a good, given to human beings by God, built on a foundation of love. The intimacy between a man and a woman is essentially a relationship of love. Not surprisingly, the Church believes that marriage is the best place for that relationship. Husband and wife give themselves to each other in many ways, including through the gift of their bodies. Without that foundation of love, men and women become *things* and not *persons*—objects rather than gifts.

RC Let's talk about the commandment in Genesis: "Be fruitful and multiply" (Gen. 1:28). This is a statement that has guided the thinking of civilization since its inception. But it seems that our brief summaries of Catholic and Jewish attitudes toward sex suggest that procreation is not the only thing we have in mind when we engage in (or think about) the act of intercourse.

JP Sexuality. The facts of life. "The birds, the bees, and the flowers." I remember before I really knew the "facts," an older friend of mine asked me why my parents had so many children

(I come from a family of ten). My response, naively, was that they loved each other. He laughed and proceeded to inform me that they were sharing a bit more than words of love to bring my siblings and me into the world. Somehow, though, I had it right, as far as the Church is concerned—my parents' love for each other was the bedrock that led them to share themselves fully with each other.

RC Do you feel that the Church taught a positive view of sexuality when you were growing up?

JP In a word, no. The Church's view of sexuality I grew up with was definitely focused on the dangers of giving in to the temptations and urges that we young people faced as we came of age. We were warned to treat our bodies as temples of God and to purge impure thoughts from our minds. That what we were experiencing was a normal part of our development as young adults wasn't communicated to us—we were made to feel guilty that we had sexual thoughts or urges. I remember being reprimanded rather sternly for dancing, in a full embrace ("clinch dancing," it was called) with my girlfriend at a Catholic high school dance. I didn't dare tell my parents about the incident. Looking back, I think the Church could have given us a more healthy understanding of sexuality as a beautiful gift of God, one reserved for the sacrament of marriage.

RC That was my understanding from all the discussions I've had with Catholic friends and colleagues over the years. But let's look at the subject more explicitly now. That is, there's the sexual relationship that warms and enhances one's marriage, and there's that *other* sex, the illicit, libidinous, explicit, "fifty shades of gray" sex that is constantly on display in the marketplace, on the Internet, and, dare I say, in the not-so-deep recesses of our consciousness. Which means, simply, that we are attracted to the other sex each time we walk out of our marital homes. Most of us, thank God, don't act on those sexual impulses, but plenty of people—men and women—do, particularly, it seems, those who hold important positions in government and society. Is that what the Church was trying to suppress, do you think, those extramarital urges even before we were married? If we were trained to control ourselves when we were single, perhaps, the Church reasoned, we would behave the way husbands and wives were supposed to behave when wedded.

JP Even after thirty-eight years of marriage, I am not immune to those impulses myself. Perhaps the Church was trying to give us a model of how we should behave in our later vocations as husbands and wives. Certainly, the temptations of the flesh don't end when we say "I do" or "I will." Today, with so many women in the workplace, the possibility for encounters that could lead a person astray has increased. And infidelity is in the news, particularly when it involves, as you mention, people in positions of power and influence. But ultimately for me, my marriage is a pact, blessed by God, between Marie and me, a total giving of ourselves to one another. We pledged to honor each other, and to seek sexual fulfillment with someone else would dishonor our vows and be an affront to the sanctity of our marriage. Succinctly put, my love for her is much greater than my lust or libido, or maybe it allows me to control or direct those normal human sexual feelings in a way God meant them to be directed.

RC That's beautifully expressed, Jerry. It's not an accident that your marriage has not only lasted for thirty-eight years, but that it continues to grow and prosper. It's that trust and confidence that you both share. You are both well aware that there are other distractions as well as seductions that are available when you walk out of your house. But you made a pledge at the time of your wedding ceremony to cherish and be faithful to each other. This means no one else enters into the privacy of your relationship. At Jewish weddings, the rabbi recites a blessing over the wine that reads: "Blessed are Thou, O Lord our God, who hast commanded us concerning forbidden connections...." The message is clear: watch out for those "forbidden connections." As we know, man, left to his instincts, will stray from what is "bidden" to what is "forbidden." Religion, and here we again get to the heart of the word itself, *binds* us to the laws that were handed down from God to Moses at Sinai. Religion protects us from straying and brings us back in line when our libidos suggest otherwise. Judaism says we have two instincts: a good inclination and an evil inclination. By the way, procreation is part of the evil inclination! Yet it is recognized that without a sexual drive "a human being would never marry, produce children, build a house, or engage in trade" (Genesis Rabbah 9:7).

So how do we balance the two? Maybe the real question is, how do we recognize that we're as liable to sin as we are to do good? That recognition, of our fallibility, is something that should have been taught better by both the Church and the Synagogue. We are susceptible to doing the "wrong thing," and the awareness of that susceptibility is critical in our efforts to follow the straight and narrow path in life. Having said all this, man does fail (I include woman in this rubric). When he or she does, we need our faith to strengthen us in the difficult times of confession and, prayerfully, reconciliation.

JP Procreation is part of the evil inclination? This idea from the same tradition that embraces the command from God to "go forth and multiply"? That took me aback at first. But in a sense, I can understand it. Something inherently good can be bad if it's misused. God's gift of sexuality certainly fits that description. We are fallible, and the realm of sexuality is one part of our humanity that proves to be a particular stumbling block for many people. Our faiths provide "road signs" to keep us on the right path and give us the strength to resist those contrary inclinations of our very human nature. Ultimately, we do believe in a God who desires to maintain a relationship with us and who can forgive our most unforgivable transgressions.

MARRIAGE

Then the Lord God said, "It is not good that the man should be alone; I will make him a helper as his partner" (Gen. 2:18).

RC Let's begin at the beginning. What do our respective faiths—Catholicism and Judaism—say about the subject of marriage?

JP Catholicism's teachings about marriage go back to Genesis, chapter 2, verse 18: "It is not good that man should be alone. I will make him a helper as his partner." Eve is that partner—bone of my bones and flesh of my flesh, Adam says—and the first marriage is the result. In marriage, a man "leaves his father and mother and clings to his wife, and they become one flesh" (Gen. 2:24). The Church considers the conjugal union of husband and wife to be a sacrament, a visible sign of God's invisible presence. The purpose of marriage, in the eyes of the Church, is twofold: first, procreation and the education of offspring ("Be fruitful and multiply"), and second, the mutual support of the spouses, each helping the other to grow in grace throughout their union together. That union is meant to be perpetual and indissoluble, a reflection of the marriage of Jesus and his Church.

RC Judaism would essentially agree, Jerry. It all begins with the biblical verse you cited—"it is not good for man to be alone." So there it is, put somewhat negatively, don't you think? But here we have it, in writing, that man needs a "helper," in order to endure all that life presents him—its joys and its difficulties. Sharing life with a chosen partner is not simply a suggestion; it is ordained. This is as important as the other commandment, seen as the first of 613 by the rabbis, to procreate. The difference in the Jewish perspective, however, may be seen in reaction to your last statement about a "perpetual and indissoluble union." Whereas Judaism promulgated the idea that marriages were entered into under the eyes of God—and actually *arranged* by Him—there was always the understanding that the marriage covenant could be negated through a divorce contract. Although we always understood that marriage was divine in origin, it could always be terminated. That is, of course another subject we will eventually address: divorce.

But let's speak personally now. I was married for eighteen years to Debbie. One beautiful child came from the relationship, our son, Josh. Yet we eventually separated and finally divorced, not because we didn't care for each other, but because the marriage was not "working" in the way each of us desired. As painful as that process was, it was necessary, I believe, because it allowed both of us to pursue a different course in our lives, resulting in what are two healthy marriages, Debbie and her husband, Ed, and my recent marriage to Jeanne.

JP Marie and I have been married for thirty-eight years. Most people would look at us and say that we have a very strong marriage, and I think we both would agree with that statement. But like any marriage, it has had its challenges—we're not one of those couples that can say we've never had an argument. Reflecting on the tenuous state of matrimony in today's society, we consider ourselves fortunate to have this bond that really has become part of who we are. I do see the spark of divinity in our marriage, just as I believe it was present in the unions of our parents. They provided wonderful examples of faith-filled mutual fidelity and sacrifice in their marriages. Marie has been a "helper" to me in so many ways, and I hope I have filled that role in her life as well. Having the blessing of two sons has also strengthened our marriage, I think. Witnessing the births of our boys was an incredible experience for me, one that brought us even closer. Perhaps that's what God intended when he said, "Be fruitful and multiply." Together, we created these children, and the shared responsibility of nurturing, teaching, and guiding them helped to strengthen the bonds between Marie and me.

RC Yes, it is clear to me that both of you have embraced the idea that God is present in our lives and particularly in our marriages. Did God pick you two to be together? Is Marie your *bashert,* your "destined one," as we say Jewishly? Predestination is a hard thing to prove. But I think a couple "needs" to believe that they were destined for each other. I think that is part of the problem today. Young people have so many different experiences (read: sexual) today that there is a real danger in thinking that marriage is just "another one" of those experiences. People wait so long to get married that, unlike our parents' generation, they don't believe in the "destiny" theory. And that makes it much easier for them to bail out of the marriage when any trouble begins. The question has changed from one of commitment to one of happiness. That is, has the institution of marriage, formerly devoted to the idea that it is a mutual commitment, devolved into the completely secular question, "Am I happy?" If we're not happy, then the conversations take a decided turn downhill. If the holiness quotient disappears from a marriage, you can be sure the marriage will as well.

JP In looking back over our thirty-eight years of marriage, I can subscribe to the belief that Marie and I were destined to be together. Our meeting, falling in love, marrying, and bringing two sons into the world was all part of God's plan for our lives. I dated other women before I met Marie, and she dated other men, but it really seems that we were meant for one another. Coming from large families, we have shared values and a mutual commitment built on a bedrock of deep faith. Am I happy? Emphatically, yes. But more important, I am very fortunate to share my life with a woman like Marie, whose love for me (and mine for her) is an enduring sign of the grace with which God has blessed our marriage. Our vows were spoken before family and friends, but also before God. With his help, we have been able to honor them all these years.

RC I remember the first time you spoke with me about Marie. You said, "Rich, I met an angel." I knew you weren't kidding. As we know, an angel is sent by God for a purpose, a mission. The qualities that Marie possesses—her kindness, her patience, her loyalty, her commitment to her faith—complement your own attributes and edify your marriage. Faith, I reiterate, is the outstanding component of your relationship. And this is what I find instructive for all of us. If our marriages are strictly formed and sustained by material means only, they most likely will not succeed. This doesn't mean that people who have no religion to fall back on will fail when they encounter the inevitable difficulties we all face in life. But…I tell couples I am fortunate enough to counsel before their wedding ceremonies that if their relationship is based only on material things, then when the marriage encounters difficulty (as it surely will), they will be facing something insurmountable as they try to get back on the right track.

The material fades. That is, despite our fascination with youth, we do age. We suffer infirmities; our children have problems; we have trouble in our careers. If we do not possess the belief that marriage *elevates* and *sanctifies* us (two words that explicitly define the two Jewish ceremonies of engagement and marriage), we are *auf tsurris*, which is a nice Yiddish saying for "in big trouble." We are so influenced by how the rest of the world lives that we often forget this covenantal relationship described in Genesis. Temptations, seductions, distractions—call them whatever you want—dissuade human beings from the real mission in life: to embrace God in our lives and to agree to love one another with all our hearts, all our souls, and all our might. And, as the first paragraph of the Shema states, "to teach them diligently to our children." In other words, the process needs to be "repeated" (which, fittingly, is also the Hebrew word for "teaching") in every generation hopefully to follow. That is our mission; that is our religious obligation.

And may all of us, parents and children, go from strength to strength and blessing to blessing.

TRADITION

Moses received the Torah from God at Mt. Sinai and passed it down to Joshua; Joshua transmitted it to the Elders; the Elders gave it to the Prophets; and the Prophets conveyed it to the Men of the Great Assembly (Sayings of the Fathers 1:1).

The Church, in its teaching, life, and worship, perpetuates and hands on to all generations all that it is itself, all that it believes (The Second Vatican Council – Dogmatic Constitution on Divine Revelation).

JP Both of our religions are steeped in traditions, which reminds me of a personal experience I had when Marie and I came down to New York to attend services at Temple Emanuel when you served there as an associate rabbi. (You were the homilist that day). As we walked down the main aisle of that beautiful temple, we found an empty pew. Instinctively, I genuflected before taking my seat. My first thought was, "I hope no one saw me do that!" After the service, Marie and I went through a receiving line where you and the other rabbis were greeting the congregants. I mentioned my "faux pas" to David Posner, your colleague, saying I hoped that it had gone unnoticed. His deadpanned response was, "I saw that." That was the last time I genuflected in a temple.

RC I remember that Sabbath! And you might know that "bending the knee" is not foreign to Judaism. Of course, your genuflecting reflected your Catholic upbringing, an act of reverence you have engaged in since you were a child. Both David Posner and I both smiled at your "pas" which was not "faux" at all. Your religious tradition is so much a part of you that you acted authentically that morning. And that is what we are speaking about—age-old traditions that inform our lives: a Passover Seder; lighting the Chanukkah Menorah; reciting the Mourner's Prayer (Kaddish) at the end of the worship service; and countless other things that identify us with our respective faiths.

JP I have always admired the traditions of Judaism and the meanings behind them. The celebrations of Christmas and Chanukkah are well known to almost every schoolchild. I can remember learning some Chanukkah songs in elementary school and learning the story of the Maccabees and the miracle of the Menorah. I didn't have many Jewish classmates, but I'm glad that our teachers gave us a glimpse into those particular traditions. As I recall, it wasn't the most ecumenical of times.

Learning the traditions of another faith is a first step to understanding and accepting those who practice it.

RC I thought the world was more ecumenical when we were growing up! But in Judaism, particularly after the 1967 and 1973 wars, we became more self-involved, unfortunately, I feel, to our detriment. But let's get specific now. We have a tradition in Judaism. In Hebrew it's called *masorah.* It means the passing on of the rites, knowledge, and commitment to the study and observance of Judaism. I always like to hearken back to the Mishnaic tractate, Sayings of the Fathers, which asserts that there are three pillars in Jewish life: "study, worship, and deeds of loving-kindness." My concern, which I often voice in sermons, is that many of us subscribe to only one-third of that prescription. At best, two-thirds. How do we become complete Jews—the answer, based on the "pillar narrative," is easy. Do all three: worship and good deeds lead to study. Study leads to worship and good deeds. And this is where both of us have noted that despite the clarity of what each tradition asks of us, congregants, parents, and children choose to do what they consider relevant in their lives. In other words, given the chance to observe and practice Judaism, most of the liberal Jewish community chooses nothing. It's a stark statement, but it is the truth.

JP Catholicism traditionally recognizes four pillars: faith, sacraments, commandments, and prayer. While many people identify themselves as Catholics, they, not unlike those "incomplete" Jews you spoke of, don't embrace all the pillars of their religion.

Attending weekend Mass is a case in point—studies reveal that about 30 percent of American Catholics fulfill that obligation. That statistic was brought home to me when I polled my religion class and found that of the dozen kids in the class, only two of them went to Mass each weekend. A disconnect is obvious—the parents send their children to religious education classes but don't reinforce the tenets of the faith they profess to believe in. For many young Catholics today, their connection with their faith culminates in and, sadly, ends with their confirmation. It's a vexing problem.

RC It's vexing to say the least. In addition, the traditional roles of priest/rabbi serving as "admonisher" of his congregation is on the edge of disappearing. As my colleague, Rabbi Posner, used to say: "They can't take it any more." But underscoring the problem is not resolving it. My interfaith colleagues in Hot Springs, Arkansas, talk constantly about inspiring belief in Jesus. And some are succeeding, at least if their numbers are an indication of success. Tell me a little more, please, about how you became so involved both with your faith and transmission of that faith within the Church and through your children.

JP Having grown up in a devoutly Catholic family certainly planted the seed of faith in me. My maternal grandmother was very spiritual in her quiet way and would often take my twin sister and me to daily Mass even before we began attending school. My parents would lead us in saying the rosary at least once a week. Sunday Mass—no Saturday liturgies in those days—was a given, along with religious instructions each week. My mother and father did their best to transmit the beliefs of their faith to all of their ten children. It must have worked, because we all have maintained our belief in God throughout our lives. I had a brief apostasy in college—I think, honestly, I was just too lazy to get out of bed and make the short walk over to the chapel—but I came back (with a bit of urging from my older brother, who was a year ahead of me in school). When I think about my faith journey, I believe that meeting and marrying Marie, who also comes from a devout Catholic family—her uncle was a priest—helped me in my spiritual growth. I'm not sure how things might have turned out if she weren't of like mind in her religious beliefs. While one's faith is a personal matter, seeing it validated in the person he loves most in this world serves to strengthen it. Perhaps, as you mentioned earlier, sharing my life and my faith with Marie was predestined. I don't have to look too far to see God's involvement in our lives—the blessings of faithful companionship and healthy children.

RC Yes, you remind me of Anthony Burgess's statement, "We are our past." You and Marie have chosen to preserve the past by "keeping the faith" in your home and transmitting it to your children. I have tried to do the same in my home and through my son, Josh. Perhaps it is different for me because Judaism was my vocation. You taught English for many years.. But perhaps the common element here is that this transmission is about teaching for both of us. Rabbi, after all, means "teacher." Has the teaching profession, being an appreciator of the *word* if you will, brought you closer to your faith?

JC Teaching English brought me great satisfaction and often joy, especially when I could help my students see the point of a story, to see a truth of human nature woven into the narrative. I think, as a species, we human beings are drawn to stories—everyone seems to like interesting, compelling ones. Is there any more compelling story than that of God and his plan for humanity? The life of Jesus has been called the greatest story ever told. The Bible, the best-selling book of all time, is one replete with stories that reveal human nature as well as divine nature. For me, teaching literature and truths about life and human nature revealed in books and stories, in "Romeo and Juliet" or *To Kill a Mockingbird* for example, have made me more open to the story of God's involvement with and plan for humanity. I hadn't thought of that connection, but I see it now, thanks to you.

RC Well, thanks. But what we have shared most deeply through all the years has been our love of words. And perhaps they all came from the Word of God. Genesis 1:1 says, "In the beginning when God created the heavens and the earth." The New Testament book of John 1:1 says, "In the beginning was the Word, and the Word was with God, and the Word was God." Divinity calls, and we respond…with faith, with commitment, with reverence for what Judaism and Christianity have given us and what we can impart to others.

JP We do indeed share a love of words. And ultimately, I believe, those words spring from a divine origin. They are a gift to us from God, meant to lead us, and those we love, to a richer, more complete relationship with him—if we only have the eyes to read them and the ears to hear them.

DISAPPOINTMENT

We know that all things work together for good for those who love God... (Rom. 8:28).

RC The topic of the day: disappointment. It's part of the human condition; we all know that. But the question is, how do we handle disappointment? Because we've all been disappointed: as children, as adolescents, as adults. And it could come in so many forms: academics, social situations, family relationships, career goals, perhaps even in our religions or, more generally, in God, who has not favored us with his blessings.

JP Certainly, disappointment is part of the human condition. We can be disappointed in and by other people, and we can be disappointed in ourselves, by what we've done or what we've failed to do. At times I've had an issue with God, wondering why the prayers I offered haven't been answered. An example that has stayed with me for more than forty years is why my prayers to restore my younger brother to health weren't heard.

His death at the age of eight rocked my faith at the time, but my disappointment and anger have been absorbed over the years by signs that make me aware that God hasn't abandoned me: a loving wife, two healthy sons, wonderful friends, a rewarding career in teaching. Those offer a counterbalance to the disappointments I've experienced in life. And perhaps, as I look back on it, suffering that loss in my teens, gave me a clearer perspective on other disappointments I've had. In a way, it gave me the strength to deal with other setbacks.

RC Yes, disappointment often leads to anger, and anger leads to resignation. And that's one of the dangers we all experience when we're disappointed. That is, if we don't recognize that disappointment is an essential part of human existence and, concomitantly, failure, then when we are invariably disappointed we lose the strength to recover our equilibrium. In my rabbinical counseling I often hear people say they don't want to venture into new relationships because they have been so disappointed in the past. It becomes "too much" for them. I can suggest, and I do, that disappointment is part of life and clearly part of every relationship we experience in life. We are disappointed in our jobs, in our spouses, in our friendships, and in our families. That happens on a daily basis. Again, we ask: what can we do either to ameliorate our situations or to not be so disappointed when we do face roadblocks and failure in our lives? How can we mitigate our disappointments, transforming unhappy thoughts and feelings into a recognition and understanding that what we experience in life is a universal condition and should be understood as so?

JP When I found myself, as a child, facing a task or a situation I didn't like, my mother would tell me, "Offer it up." She was encouraging me to accept the unpleasant situation in imitation of Jesus Christ, who offered himself up to death for the sins of humanity. How disappointed Jesus must have been in his closest friends, yet he still offered himself in expiation for their shortcomings and those of all mankind. As Catholics, we are taught to unite our disappointments and sufferings with those of Christ, rather than to shake our fist at God or at other people. These angry responses to disappointment could lead to bitterness and alienation, it seems to me.

RC *Imitatio dei,* "in imitation of God." Our traditions, Christianity and Judaism, although they take different paths to repentance, do, as your mom said, "Offer it up." The High Holy Days Liturgy admonishes us, through endless recounting of our sins, to amend our behavior and achieve forgiveness by recognizing the validity of our neighbor's feelings as well as our own. I love the wisdom of William James, the less famous James brother, who said: "Joy is joy, pain is pain, everywhere, even as in thee." We interact with other people all the time; therefore, they do have influence on our life and, in many cases, their behavior can affect our lives adversely. However, we do not always recognize that we inflict pain equally upon *them.* By examining our own actions, and by seeking out those we have offended—a prime activity for Jews during the Holy Day period—we can let go of much of our disappointment and anger and move forward, taking more responsibility for our behavior as we take renewed positive steps, with God's help, in our lives.

JP In the Lord's Prayer, we ask God to "forgive us our trespasses as we forgive those who trespass against us." None of us is perfect, and we are also sometimes blind to how we may have offended or disappointed others. We need to be reconciled with those who have somehow disappointed or hurt us. To do so is a reflection of the Divinity who created us, who wants to maintain a relationship with us, and who is willing to forgive even our most grievous transgressions. God, no doubt, has ample reason to be disappointed in the actions of his human creations, but as we witness in the Old Testament, he deeply desires to maintain a covenant with his people, despite their hardheartedness and apostasy. Similarly, we cannot allow our dark moments or disappointments to sever our ties to our fellow human beings or to God. Rather, we need to seek God's help, as you mentioned, to accept those experiences as part of what it means to be a human being.

RC But as the Beatles have said: "You know it ain't easy." And to rehash an old theme, who said it would be? We were lucky to have the parents we did, Jerry. Or maybe it was the generation in which we grew up, as heirs to "the greatest generation." Mom and Dad were sympathetic when I experienced disappointment as a child, but they were not overly sympathetic! That is the key for those mothers and fathers today who believe that their children should never face disappointment in their lives. "In their lives!" How about the disappointment we experience every day? We cannot protect ourselves nor our children from the troubles that arise daily—in our jobs, in our relationships, and in our quashed dreams. How do we cope with these regular defeats? How do we deal with our inability to have what we want in our lives? The answer, the religious answer, does not mitigate the fact that we will be disappointed. Rather, religion helps us to understand that *when* we are disappointed, we will find the strength to continue our life paths with optimism. Disappointment will come, as sure as day turns into night, but belief and commitment to our respective faiths can distill our hurts and wounds, allowing us to return once again to our secular lives, better students of the human condition and more capable of internalizing both the good and bad in ourselves and in society. Think disappointments are difficult to handle? How about when those disappointments turn into *failures,* a word that has been removed from our households today—as if it would be too damaging to articulate aloud before and to those whom we love. I think we need to spend some time with *failure,* Jerry. It is as much or even more a part of the human condition as *success.*

FAILURE

No one who conceals transgressions will prosper, but one who confesses and forsakes them will obtain mercy (Prov. 28:13).

RC Our topic today: *failure*. It's a word each of us grew up with; it's a term of art our parents were not afraid to confront us with; it's something each of us knows, if we have any real perception about the course of our lives. The ability to admit we have failed may not be popular in a world filled with so many excuses today, but understanding the nature of our failures allows each of us true religious insight and, hopefully, the ability to correct, amend, and change our behavior so that we may become successful—that is, lead better, more ethical and honest lives.

JP Failure, one saying has it, is an event, and not a person. To be human is to be imperfect, and such events are part of everyone's life. The spectrum of failure is a wide one. We sometimes fail to do what we should or to say what we should; we fail in our relationships with other people, in our jobs, in our resistance to temptations and evil. A recognition of our failures is the first step to the change in behavior you speak of; that and a belief that God wants us to be better versions of ourselves, that failure does not have to have the final word. The Catholic Church offers the Sacrament of Reconciliation as a way of redressing one's personal failures. Admittedly, the number of Catholics availing themselves of that particular sacrament has fallen precipitously in recent times. But it remains a means by which failure can be transmuted into something that leads to a deeper understanding of self and what God wants for us—to be the better, more ethical people you speak of.

RC This Sacrament of Reconciliation: are you speaking of the Confessional?

JP Yes, the Confessional is the place where Catholics give an accounting of their transgressions or failures, ask for forgiveness, and are granted absolution by the confessor. It's one of two means by which Catholics admit to and seek forgiveness for their failure to follow God's commandments and teachings of the Church. The other means is a rite that occurs at the beginning of the Catholic Mass: we recite the *Confiteor*, a communal prayer in which we confess our faults (*Confiteor* means "I confess" in Latin) and ask God to forgive us for "what we have done, and what we have failed to do." These are sins of commission and omission, both failures in a real sense.

This communal prayer is not meant to take the place of reconciliation or confession. The sacrament allows the penitent to seek God's grace in order to avoid errant behavior in the future. That's one way of looking at failure and responding to it, although you may have had a more "catholic" view in mind with the term.

RC Perhaps I did at the beginning of the discussion. But the more I think about it, there seems to be some correspondence between "sins" and "failures." On the Jewish High Holy Days, we recite a litany of verses that begin with the words *Al chet,* literally "For the sin." An example: "For the sin which we have sinned against Thee by disrespect for parents and teachers; For the sin which we have sinned against Thee in stubbornness or in error." We tend to separate "failure" from "sin," but it seems to me that the two words do belong together. Do we sin in our marriages, in our careers, in our relationships by violating the codes of behavior expected of us in those respective situations? Does sin bring us to failure? Does failure bring us to sin? These are not easy questions. We have spoken about the subject of sin in a separate conversation. But as we move forward with more specific examples of failure, it may behoove us to remember that there is an undeniable theological connection here.

That being understood, let's speak more secularly now. We each fail every day of our lives. We fail to attain the goals we set for ourselves in our careers. We fail to please our spouses in our marriages. My first marriage failed. That failure, and the trauma of that failure, resulted in a mere eighteen-year hiatus for me until I married Jeanne almost five years ago. My career as a rabbi, once a smooth and untroubled arc at Temple Emanu-El in New York, swerved toward three other venues—in Greenwich for eight years, West Palm for three years, and now Hot Springs, Arkansas, for the last three. These are not just bumps in the road; they have caused me great anguish and difficulty in my life. The issue becomes how to evaluate these failures. First, one needs to recognize the failure. So many people have told me that I didn't fail in my marriage. I immediately respond, "No, I *did* fail!" That seems to shock them. But owning up to your failure is something I learned as a child in the house of Lila and Harold Chapin. There are of course the little failures—the bad marks on tests, the inability to get a hit for your team, the inattentiveness when your wife is saying something to you – there are surely a million of these examples. Those are easier to acknowledge. But it's the big ones you've got to watch out for—they can do you in if you don't have a practical and honest way of dealing with them.

JP I knew Debbie very well, having first met her when you began dating back in our college days. Frankly, to hear you say you failed in your marriage to her is unsettling. I guess I'm among that group of your friends who believe that you didn't fail, but rather that things *didn't work out.* I suspect that that particular expression, in your mind, might be a euphemism for failing. So I understand and respect that for you, the dissolving of your marriage was a failure. And the acceptance of that failure—along with the causes of it—can only make you strive to ensure that you avoid such an experience in the future.

RC Yes, well said. But all the assurance (or reassurance) in the world doesn't mean you won't fail again. And I do appreciate the comforting words: it "just didn't work out." That is the result. But it raises a larger question: what is our responsibility in a marriage? Sometimes a confrontation with a spouse can be a good thing—"clearing the air." I lacked, at that time, the ability to confront Debbie, and so I sat there, hoping over the years that certain things would get better. But there was a hole in our marriage that, in effect, mitigated our ability to heal the wounds we had inflicted upon each other. I had my gripes; she had hers. We went to counseling; we remained considerate of each other. I always had, and continue to have, deep respect for her intelligence. But parting ways enabled both of us to reevaluate our lives and, eventually, to find new partners. We each have another chance now with new spouses and new families. But my goodness, Jerry, it took a long time for me to consider marriage as a happy option once again. As to my continuously flawed condition and my new sets of failures, well, the difference is that now I am comfortable admitting them and speaking about them to Jeanne (and she about hers), as we bump along together into the good night.

Let me ask you a question now: You've been married nearly thirty-eight years; you have been a lifelong English teacher at the same school, you've raised two wonderful boys with Marie. You've fortunately missed out on some of those big failures. So…where do you see yourself with respect to our subject?

JP An example of failure in my own life, one of commission, took place during my junior high school years. I was relatively sheltered and not very "streetwise" when it came to the facts of life in elementary school. When I entered junior high, I met some kids who were more advanced than I was, and I fell under their influence. At their prodding, I wrote some entries containing obscenities and sexual references, some of which I didn't really understand at the time, in a small autograph book being circulated among the group. Unfortunately for me, my father was a guidance counselor at my junior high, and when a teacher confiscated the book, it eventually ended up in my father's hands. I knew I was in trouble.

I'll never forget our conversation when he questioned me about whether I had written some of the offensive comments in the book. Not wanting to compound my transgression with a lie, I told him I had. His response, which pierced more deeply than any other could have, was, "You're no son of mine!" I had failed to live up to my father's standard of behavior, and he was deeply disappointed in me. My father's approval meant a great deal to me, and I don't think he could have spoken any other words that could have affected me more deeply. Even now, fifty years later, they haven't lost their sting. Though I'm sure my dad probably forget the incident—I never brought it up with him in later years—I think of it as an example of personal failure, specifically failure to be the person my parents had taught me to be. And I learned something about myself and the danger of bending to other people's ideas of how I should conduct myself.

RC What a powerful memory, Jerry. And what an effect your father's chastisement had upon your life. I hearken back to all the times my mother said things to me that hurt my feelings but were true. Dad was not the spokesperson in our home. Years later, after chastising my son, Josh, for something he had done (this may have happened fewer than five times in his twenty-seven year-old existence), I called my mother because I was feeling guilty. I asked, "Mom, you used to reprimand us all the time for things we had done wrong. Did you ever feel guilty about it?" Without a pause, she said, "No, I said what I had to say and moved on." I laughed and replied, "Well, we didn't."

And that may be the major difference we see today in how we deal with our and our children's failures in life. Our parents saw what we had done incorrectly in our daily lives, and they did not hesitate to amend our behavior—*immediately.* We, armed with books and words designed to help us "cope with" our family's problems, have bent so far backward to make sure we are not "damaging" the egos of our children that we often miss the mark. And so, when we do something bad or fail in our quest to be ethical, even noble people, instead of owning up to what is wrong with our behavior we find excuses, alibis, and rationalizations for our children and for ourselves. In the "old" days, when a teacher told me that I wasn't performing in the way he or she liked, my mother first chastised me, and then we made an appointment with the instructor so that I could be straightened out. Today, and you certainly know this as a lifelong teacher, the mother will come in to the school and chastise the teacher for not understanding the "special" qualities her child possesses. You are failing the student; it's not the other way around.

But after the acres of accumulated wisdom in all those self-help tomes I have tried to assiduously avoid in the bookstores, I think this story about Murph Pitarresi (your inimitable father) speaks volumes in that one-sentence reprimand: "You're no son of mine!" He, like my mom and dad, had standards, and when we weren't meeting them, there was no hesitation in reminding us where we stood—that is, we *didn't* stand without their support. We knew that, and having been chastised, we responded with better efforts.

Failure: it's a word no one wants to hear, but if we do not have the courage to admit we fail, we are merely "pretend" husbands and wives, fathers and mothers, unable to uphold the standards that were set for us in our original homes.

ANGER

Those who are hot-tempered stir up strife, but those who are slow to anger calm contention (Prov. 15:18).

RC Our topic today: anger. Is there a subject that plagues us more in our lives? Well, I know you love word play. Here's some Hebrew word play. The rabbis of late antiquity said that one can tell the true nature of a human being *kiso, koso, and kaaso*, "by his wine cup, by his purse, and by his anger." You can almost hear a textual caesura. Then the rabbis continue: "But the greatest difficulty man faces is his anger." The other *symbols—kiso* and *koso—pertain* to man's generosity. How charitable is he to the community? How welcoming and hospitable is he to the guest in his home?

So let's take another moment to recognize, as two religionists must, that the God of the Bible most certainly possessed the attribute of anger. Perhaps, then, we need a two-pronged approach to our topic.

JP The God of the Old Testament could show anger, to be sure. The disobedience of Adam and Eve and the apostasy of his Chosen People provoked his ire, and rightfully so, I might add. That God is capable of anger shouldn't surprise us—Catholics believe that human beings are made in the image and likeness of God; if we can display anger, cannot God do the same? Perhaps seeing the God of the Old Testament as Father makes his anger seem more acceptable. He has good reason to be upset with his children, his creations, who turned away from him despite all he had done for them.

RC Yes, there are countless examples in the Bible of Israel's provocation of God. It reaches the point, particularly in the forty-year sojourn in the desert, at which Moses stays the hand of God's anger as God is ready to erase his creation from its earthly confines. And we know, do we not, that Jesus had a temper as well?

JP Yes, he did; the first time I read about his anger exploding in the scene where he drives the buyers and sellers out of the Temple, I was shocked. It seemed out of character for this man who spoke of love, forgiveness, and peace to act with such fury. But again, he was human as well as divine, and the anger he displayed was self-righteous—his Father's house was being turned into a shopping mall, and he could not allow that defilement. Having my own experiences with anger, I can empathize with Jesus in this scene.

RC I think that's quite helpful. We must recognize that anger is part of the human experience; it is as real and understandable as its concomitant, happiness. In my career I have been amazed to see how many people are much more in touch with their anger than they are with what brings them joy in life. The rabbis tell us that Moses possessed an abundance of patience with his people; in addition, he was viewed as the most humble person ever created. But as I see it, he had trouble with his temper. Before his career as Israel's leader ever began, he killed an Egyptian. He often lamented about his difficult task of commanding the Israelites. And let us not us forget the "smiting of the rock" not once but twice, when he could have gently tapped it to produce water. I have turned more often to the example of Abraham, who, I would argue, has much better control of his anger than the great Moses. Abraham's life, a life devoted to welcoming the stranger—keeping the tent flaps open in every direction—accepting all peoples into that tent, is the most exemplary of any biblical figure. It's not that Abraham did not have a temper. As mentioned earlier, we all do! It's his exemplary control of his temper that impresses me the most and makes me want to emulate his character.

JP Anger is one of the famed Seven Deadly Sins, popularized by European artists and by Dante in the *Divine Comedy* during the Middle Ages. The Catholic Church uses the term *capital sins.* We have to be careful to differentiate between two kinds of anger: righteous anger, or indignation, and unjust anger, which has no justifiable cause. Bishop Fulton J. Sheen, in writing on the Seven Deadly Sins, refers to unjust anger as something that is "excessive, revengeful, or enduring…or that seeks to repay in kind." Jesus was very angry with the buyers and sellers in Temple, but he had justification for that strong emotion: they were defiling his Father's house. Conversely, I'm not justified in reacting with road rage over someone cutting me off in traffic, unless perhaps that person has put me or another driver at risk of being harmed.

RC I'm very taken with Bishop Sheen's statement about "unjust anger." We all have irrational sides that cause us to misinterpret the motives of others. Indeed, road rage is a good example. We tend to think that those who cut us off or drive dangerously have a personal grudge against us. (Are we perhaps driving too nice a car for their taste?) There are hundreds of things we imagine that other people think, but ultimately it is our reaction to the so-called offense that is most important. Road rage endangers us more than our imagined highway adversaries. This is supported by the many accidents that result from our anger. I would submit that even if that person has put us in danger, it is our obligation to pull back, both physically and emotionally from seeking to "repay in kind." That is not easy, but that I believe is what the Bishop is suggesting. How do we turn irrational behavior into rational behavior? That is a difficult question, because we all have "anger thresholds." Yet truly our lives, how we live our lives, depend on it.

JP I can endorse your idea of an anger threshold. Recognizing it and turning potentially irrational behavior into rational behavior is more in line with what the Church teaches about dealing with anger. I had an experience recently that speaks to anger and how to respond to it. Marie and I are die-hard Buffalo Bills fans, and we attended several of their home games this past season. After one of the games, unfortunately a loss, we were making our way to our car. While we were waiting to cross a street, a Bills fan next to us started chanting an obscenity about the opposing team. My ten-year-old nephew was with us, along with his father, and I wasn't pleased that young Christopher and my wife had to be subjected to such behavior. I bit my tongue, however, and even told a man next to me, garbed in the jersey of the opposing team, not to react for fear that some violence would erupt.

My fears were justified—I lost track of the offensive Bills fan for a moment, but then I suddenly saw him again along with several other men in the middle of the street. It was an ugly scene—fists were flying wildly and the Bills fan punched another guy two or three times. I watched, anger swelling inside me, as the victim of the beating fell and lay motionless in the roadway. My first instinct was to run out and try to restrain the assailant, a reaction fueled perhaps by a girl I didn't know screaming at me, "You have to do something!" I hollered for the police and started to run out into the street, not sure whether to help the unconscious victim or try to throw myself at the aggressor, who was much bigger and younger than I. Anger and adrenalin were telling me to do something, but luckily, my wife helped me to act in a more reasoned way. Marie pulled me back, no doubt saving me from physical harm. My brother-in-law and I were able to get the police to the scene, report to them what we had witnessed, and watch as they arrested the Bills fan as he attempted to leave the scene in a car driven by some friends. Ultimately, what we did was the most effective way to deal with the ugly situation. I have to credit Marie for making me take a more rational approach, though I'm sure she was most concerned about my physical well-being.

RC She was concerned for you, and rationally so. Thank God. But your story does show that we're all capable of anger, and although I applaud you for your decision to become involved (so many of us would avoid that vulgar scene like the plague), I take note at your first instinct, which might have caused you serious harm or injury. Part of me admires your courage, because I would have repressed that first instinct to get into the melee. You were rightfully upset and angered by that so-called fan (and we know these "fans" are spoiling games for decent people in every NFL venue). You acted out of conviction, another positive thing. But…how far are we meant to go in these matters? You and I are sixty-four years old now, and while we arguably are in excellent condition, it is more than likely we would get the worst of it in a fight with a much younger man. Truth is, dear friend, I haven't even had the inclination to engage in fisticuffs with anyone since high school. A few years ago, I was verbally abused by a leader in my congregation, who was dissatisfied with the way I was performing as a rabbi. Unfortunately, this was not someone who had any appreciation of my character and my sincere concern for the community. Over the months, his chastisements became accusations, and the accusations became threats. It turned the atmosphere so black between us that I dreaded meeting him. Once, after an angry lunch filled with recriminations, I tried to escape from him by walking to my car. He accosted me, saying, "When you leave another person, you should look him in the eyes and shake his hand." For the first time in my adult life, I realized that I was close to engaging another person physically.

That incident had serious consequences. A long period of threats, lawyers, and angry repercussions followed. I was terribly angry. But I suffered that anger in private. I let the lawyer take care of the rest. What I experienced is not unique. My anger was justified, but I knew that I had to control the situation before I did something that would be the antithesis of why I became a rabbi in the first place. I remain thankful that it was resolved, but I don't think I could ever speak with my offender again.

JP My experiences with anger and its consequences in my life have taught me that I need to be better at dealing with it. I think prayer helps, along with an understanding that other people deserve more forbearance from me, simply because I don't know what may have prompted the behavior that provokes my ire. If I truly believe in the teachings of my faith, I have to turn the other cheek and not respond in kind. That might be difficult, but it's what Christ commanded his followers to do.

RC We all do, Jerry. Religious principles and religious practice can help us deal with the things that get our goats. But controlling our temper is, as always, something that needs constant work. When we bring our anger home after frustrating days in the office and deal with that anger either through abuse of alcohol or, worse, abuse of our families, we are committing a sin against the commandment known as *shalom bayit,* or "keeping peace in the home." The subject runs very deep and affects every aspect of our existence. Let us pray for the strength to fulfill our promises to those whom we love, and those who share our communities.

TEMPTATION OF THE FLESH

And do not bring us to the time of trial, but rescue us from the evil one (Matt. 6:13).

JP As Catholics, we recite the Our Father at every Mass. The prayer ends with the following petition: "And lead us not into temptation, but deliver us from evil." We acknowledge that the world has ways of leading us astray, and we ask God's help in turning away from the siren call of various temptations. I start each day with a prayer called the Lorica or St. Patrick's Breastplate. It asks for "God's shield to protect me, and God's host to secure me—against snares of devils, against temptations and vices, against inclinations of nature." The point of both prayers is that we humans can't go it alone; we need God's help, his grace, to prevent us from yielding to the potentially destructive allurements that we encounter every day. And the reference to the devil is instructive, because in Catholic teaching, Satan and other evil beings doing his bidding are believed to exist. The battle is waged every day in each of us.

RC I am very taken with these shield images, both in the Latin word *Lorica* and St. Patrick's Breastplate. A *shield* is a literal object that of course has become symbolic for worshippers today. When the traditional Jew wakes up in the morning, he puts on his prayer phylacteries. These two small black boxes are called *tefillin* and contain four biblical passages taken from the books of Exodus and Deuteronomy. One of those passages states: "Keep these words that I am commanding you this day...bind them as a sign on your hand, fix them on your forehead, and write them on the doorposts of your house and on your gates" (Deut. 6:6–9). This literal binding keeps us close to God's commandments. When we remove these *tefillin* from our left arm, a visible imprint of that binding period remains—those commandments to obey God and resist temptation are still with us.

We need literal signs to keep us in line. Indeed, Judaism has the *Magen David*, or "Shield of David," on which you'll find the six-pointed star. David certainly had many problems with temptation, but the symbol of the Jewish Star, which is emblazoned on the Israeli flag, has inspired countless generations of Jews to "keep the faith."

JP How to "keep the faith"? Of course, we have the Ten Commandments as *the* guidelines for following the path God wants us to walk. Seeking strength to avoid temptation through prayer is another means afforded us. We pray for strength to the saints of the church, many of whom who were faced with the same worldly temptations. In Catholicism we can also draw support from our belief that Jesus, sharing in our fully human nature, faced temptations in his own life. We can turn to Jesus and appeal to him for help in resisting the temptations we face in our lives. And we have the solace of knowing that if we succumb to these weaknesses of the flesh, we can ask for forgiveness and renew our resolve to resist evil in the sacrament of Reconciliation. These are not fool-proof, ironclad ways of avoiding evil, but they can help build that shield that can protect us in the ongoing conflict between our propensity for evil and our desire to be the best person we can be.

RC I was taught in rabbinical school that the more difficult a commandment was to observe, the more safeguards we put around it. The monks were onto something when they decided to live in caves. Avoid temptation by avoiding any contact with society. Try living in society and doing the same. The 2013 Super Bowl showcased the talents, both artistic and lascivious, of Beyoncé. Many playfully suggested that the power outage that occurred following the halftime show was the result of her not infrequent "bumps and grinds." How do we safeguard against *that*? Do we just shake our heads, admit the obvious—i.e., that she is a symbol of sexiness—and move back into our protective shells? Temptation surrounds us in every aspect of our lives. Knowing that we will be tempted is a surety. The question remains: how do we handle it? Because we know, dear Jerry, that all the prayers and bindings of our faiths notwithstanding, we have been and we will be continually challenged by the world of seduction.

JP We are certainly not immune to the world of seduction. It's ubiquitous today. My subscription to *Sports illustrated* includes the annual swimsuit issue—tame by today's standards, but still trading on one of the basic truths in the world of publishing: sex sells. And not surprisingly. Sexuality is part of our makeup as human beings. In our younger years, Richard, we both enjoyed the company of attractive women. Years later, our marriages to two wonderful women don't blind us to the attractiveness of other females. We can see them, but how we respond to what we see is the key. I know that my love for my wife and my pledge to honor and obey her, made thirty-eight years ago before family, friends, and God, are more important to me and give me the strength to deal with temptations of the flesh.

RC Everyone who reads the Bible dwells on the story of the seduction of Eve and Adam by the "cunning serpent." It is a classic narrative on the origin of *temptation*. Yet for those of us who dwell in the fleshpots of modernity, I would submit that the narrative of Joseph tells us not only how we succumb to temptation, but more important, how we can overcome it. Remember Joseph? He was an early version of Freud, a master of dreams. His early dreams got him into big trouble with his brothers, who threw him into a pit. Remarkably resilient, after being hijacked to Egypt, Joseph arose to prominence in Pharaoh's court. Unfortunately, this gregarious young man, who the Bible says, "was handsome of form and handsome of appearance," attracts the attentions of an Egyptian minister's wife. The temptress brazenly says to him, "Lie with me." The text then reads, "But he refused," a clear and swift rebuke to his seductress. His dignity is preserved. But not so fast. A wavering musical sign over the Hebrew word for "he refused" is interpreted by generations of commentators as a sign of Joseph's indecisiveness. Should he indulge in forbidden sexual relations with this would-be adulterer? That he was attracted to her is obvious. But committing a sin—that gave him pause. According to the rabbis in the Midrash, Joseph was prepared to engage in sexual relations with Potiphar's wife, but at the last moment, he saw images before him of the patriarchs, Abraham, Isaac, and his own father, Jacob. Their appearance at this perilous moment suggests to the aroused youth that if he should engage in the sexual act he will lose his future standing as one of the great patriarchs of the Jewish people. And he doesn't! Indeed, now chastened by his ancestors, he says to the temptress, "My master…has denied me nothing but you, since you are his wife; how then can I perpetrate this great evil and sin against God!"

Joseph's conclusion helps settle our discussion on temptation. We all have opportunities in life to be unfaithful to our partners. Stories of sexual infidelity are the rule, not the exception. But sexual fidelity? That's the real challenge today, especially when the opportunity to stray seems readily available in every direction and in every location. If we do not have a higher calling; if we do not see ourselves as safeguarding something sacred; if we see the world only in material terms—then our marriages will founder. We, like our precious possessions, will lose our youthful luster. If we do not see a religious calling in our marriages, we will find it extremely easy to incline our heads to something or someone who is *seductive, exciting,* and, perhaps most important, not the *same person* to whom we once pledged to dedicate our lives. We can't snuff out temptation, but we can, and we must, find a way to live with it.

OTHER TEMPTATIONS

JP As I write this, Catholics and other Christians have just entered the forty days of Lent, a spiritual journey that begins with Ash Wednesday. While we don't go around wearing sackcloth anymore, we Catholics are easy to pick out on this first day of Lent because of the ashes, in the form of a cross, that the priest places on our foreheads. As he marks us with the ashes, a symbol of our mortality and our need for repentance and spiritual renewal, the priest says, "Remember that you are dust and unto dust you shall return." That invocation echoes the Genesis story of God's creation of Adam and Eve from the dust of the earth, their prideful disobedience, and their subsequent fall from grace. It reflects, as well, our own shared fallen nature.

Lent's length of forty days commemorates Jesus's fasting in the desert for that length of time in preparation for his mission to bring the news of the Kingdom of God to the world.

Commingled with the story of Jesus's sojourn in the desert is that of his tempting by the devil, a dramatic lesson in resistance to evil for all of us (see Luke 4:1–14 and Matthew 4).

We might expect that after such a prolonged fast, Jesus, whom Catholics believe truly shared our human nature while also being truly divine, would have been both very hungry and thirsty. Enter the devil, who is aware of Jesus's weakened state and tries to entice Jesus into pledging his fealty to him rather than to God the Father. Satan first issues a challenge to Jesus, saying that if he is truly the Son of God, he should turn a stone to bread and thus satisfy his hunger. Jesus rejects that proposal out of hand, saying, "One does not live by bread alone, but by every word that comes from the mouth of the Lord" (Matt. 4:4). Then Satan tempts Jesus by saying he will give him dominion over all the kingdoms of the earth if only Jesus will worship the Prince of Darkness. Once again, Jesus rejects the devil's offer, saying the only one we are to worship is the Lord, our God. In the climax to the drama, Satan once again challenges Jesus to prove his divinity ("*If* you are the Son of God") by flinging himself off the parapet of the temple, "for it is written: 'He (God) will command his angels concerning you, to guard you…With their hands they will support you, lest you dash your foot against a stone.'" Jesus summarily dismisses the devil by saying "It (Scripture) also says, 'You shall not put the Lord, your God, to the test.'" The devil, unsuccessful in his quest, departs, as the passages concludes, "for a time."

Luke's Gospel is instructive. Like Jesus, we all have our own "desert" experiences, times when we are most vulnerable to the assaults of temptation, whether they emanate from desires of the flesh and the material world or from pride. And while we may prove equal to the test in one instance, we can't let down our guard—the devil may leave for a time, as the Scripture says, but we can be sure he, along with his temptations, will return.

Temptations surround us every day—in the workplace and in our private spaces. Alexander Woollcott, like both of us, Richard, an alumnus of Hamilton College, once wrote, "All the things I really like to do are either illegal, immoral, or fattening." No doubt many people can empathize with Woollcott. How can we resist temptations? Recognizing when we are most vulnerable or susceptible to them is a start. Doing something concrete to prevent the enticements from taking hold of us, being *proactive* in today's parlance, can be beneficial. The three actions that Catholics are especially encouraged to follow during Lent—prayer, fasting, and almsgiving—can be efficacious in turning someone away from temptation, I think. They can lead us to a deeper, fuller relationship with God and enable us to focus outward rather than inward, on others rather than on ourselves. These three "pillars" can help us live by the two commandments Jesus considered the most important of all: first, to love God with our whole heart, our whole soul, our whole mind, and our whole strength; and next, to love our neighbors as ourselves. If we examine our actions, Richard, using those two commandments (would you call them Mitzvahs?) as our lens, we might well, in the words of the Our Father, not be led "into temptation," but rather, our choices will be ones that indeed "deliver us from evil."

We are human, and we will face temptations. That's a fact of life. Through God's grace, we can find the strength to resist them and follow the commandment the Lord enjoined Moses to give to the people of Israel, to "be holy; for I the LORD your God am holy" (Lev. 19:2). The path God wants us to follow is clear; the choice to do so or not remains ours. Not unlike the situation our first parents found themselves in, don't you think?

RC You've written a beautiful piece, Jerry. Deeply theological, to be sure. It's funny, but I keep thinking about chapter 12 of the *Odyssey,* in which Odysseus lashes himself to his ship's mast in order to resist the call of the Sirens. You remember that he orders all his shipmates to stuff their ears with beeswax so that they can watch over him without being lured into the rock-infested waters lurking beneath those femmes fatales. But one might ask, why didn't Odysseus stuff his own ears with that protective wax? The more I consider the passage, the more I'm convinced that he didn't mute his ears because he *wanted* to be tempted by the Sirens. That is, he wanted to feel "the Particulars of Rapture." I've put those words in quotes because they happen to serve as the title to Aviva Zornberg's masterful commentary on the book of Exodus. There's rapture that is acquired through the physical senses; there's rapture that is acquired through spiritual apprehension. We have spoken about the Jewish prayer ritual in which men don leather phylacteries that at once symbolize and speak of being bound to the commandments of Torah. Torah binds us to its eternal precepts, but its narrative acknowledges the constant temptations we experienced in the wilderness and the many times we succumbed to those temptations—whether cavorting with members of the wrong tribes (read: gentiles), or building a golden calf because we did not believe Moses would return from Mt. Sinai, or looking for Manna on the Sabbath after we had already received a double portion on Friday.

Here is a little linguistic play for a dear friend who loves plays on words. When students study the commentary on the Bible, known generally as Talmud but more familiarly called *Gemara,* they speak of the *daf* they are parsing. *Daf* means "page." Each page has an A and B side. But *daf* also means "plank." The rabbis tell us that we must hold onto our Torah as dearly as if we had found a plank to buoy us up after being shipwrecked in the ocean. That image of being rescued by a mast or plank of wood is thematically suggested in Gericault's *Raft of the Medusa.* More famously, in *Moby Dick,* the forlorn orphan, Ishmael, holds on to Queequeg's coffin for dear life until he is rescued by a ship, "the devious-cruising Rachel," named for the beloved mother of the Jewish exile.

I see another image of the "plank." That piece of wood is a source of life; it provides succor and salvation. It is not an accident that Christian scholars have seen Isaac, who carries the wood up to the sacrificial altar, as a prototype for Jesus's bearing his cross to Golgotha. The cross, for Christians, is their "mast," their "plank." Each *daf,* each "page" of the New Testament brings one closer to understanding the rationale for viewing him as the Messiah. His forty-day trial in the wilderness demonstrates that even he endured temptation. But he, as did Moses, rejected any assumption of power that was a usurpation of God's authority. Ultimately, both leaders were as humble as they were righteous.

We lesser mortals, who try to resist the seductions of Sirens in this world, must turn to our respective traditions for strength in the face of temptation. We must cling to our *daf,* both the "page" and the "plank," in order to remain faithful to all the promises we have made to our fellow human beings, and to God.

FORGIVENESS

The gates of repentance are always open (Pesikta of Rav Kahana, p. 142b).

RC Let's talk about forgiveness. I read a piece in the *New York Times* today by Alina Tugend that dealt with our ability to forgive people for their transgressions...even people we do not know. Clearly a multitude of famous people of late have felt the need to make public apologies for their actions in the hope that they might reclaim our affection. We sit in thrall at celebrities who reveal their "sinful" behavior to talk show hosts—usually Oprah. The narratives of Tiger Woods and Lance Armstrong head the list. Implicitly called upon is the human instinct to forgive the formerly unblemished hero his sins so that we may worship at his feet once again. Ms. Tugend cites a book by Jeremy D. Holden, *Second That Emotion* (2012), that suggests the reason we care so much about the behavior of our heroes is that we "develop a 'social contract' with them that is based not on logic, but rather on the mistaken belief that we actually understand them because we hear and read about them so much." Jeffrie Murphy, professor of law, philosophy, and religious studies at Arizona State University, submits that the entire concern to forgive our "celebrity sinners" is an illusion. Because we have a "fantasy image" of these athletic paragons, we feel let down by them.

We all know the aphorism, "To err is human, to forgive divine." We know we are supposed to forgive those who wrong us, and yet how far do we take this principle? It is one thing to forgive another who has hurt us. But if the injury is serious, can we move past "forgiveness" to "trust?" I know, Jerry, that there are incidents in my life where I have recognized that I felt hurt and also chose to hurt another person in retaliation. In some cases I was able to transition from forgiveness to a level of trust. But in other cases, I chose to walk away from the relationships, knowing that I could not fully trust them again. Maybe this comes under the rubric "forgive and forget." The saint-like person will fully forgive the person who sinned against him and will open his heart with trust that they can begin their relationship anew. But others of us cannot forget the wrong and thus cannot move forward.

JP Forgiving those who have hurt or wronged us is a teaching of Jesus that all Christians are enjoined to follow. And to use the popular phrase, he didn't just talk the talk, he walked the walk, carrying his cross to Calvary, and in the throes of his excruciatingly painful death, beseeching God, "Father, forgive them; they know not what they do." Can we then do any less? In the Gospel of Matthew, Jesus preaches, "Love your enemies, and pray for those who persecute you, that you may be children of your heavenly Father." Ultimately, we are all sinners, and we all benefit from the unconditional forgiveness of God. Forgiving and forgetting might not be possible, but truly forgiving another person is an act that frees us to be the loving people God wants us to be. We're human, and feelings of anger and resentment and a desire to "get even" can be stumbling blocks to forgiveness. But Jesus gave us the road map to achieving it in his willingness to forgive those who tortured and crucified him, as well as in his famous commandments to "turn the other cheek" when others do something to hurt us and to love our neighbors as ourselves. With God's grace, we can find our way to forgiveness and love of all humanity...even those we may find unlovable.

RC Those are exquisite thoughts. Perhaps the best thing about forgiving our adversaries is the release of the bad feelings, including guilt, that haunt us before the reconciliation occurs. And yet, as suggested earlier, we cannot always complete the process—that is, first forgiving and then trusting. Some people find great satisfaction in not forgiving a person they consider to be the guilty party. Indeed, Judaism, as evidenced in Leviticus 19:17, admonishes us to admonish others when they do wrong: "Thou shalt surely admonish." Our greatest scholar in Jewish history, Maimonides, emphasizes our need to chastise and rebuke the person who has wronged us. If we do not, says Maimonides, then *we* are the guilty party! It's a delicate process, forgiveness. Chastising someone who has done wrong may be the prerequisite. Will chastisement lead to reconciliation? I was certainly chastised plenty of times in my own household. It seemed to be my obligation to accept that rebuke and become reconciled to it. It certainly didn't seem to be my parents' problem. Love, then, beginning with biblical love, is surely conditional. If we meet God's standards, then we merit his love. If not, well, we all know what happened to the Israelites when the Lord was displeased.

JP In the Our Father, a prayer Jesus taught his disciples and one that is recited at every Mass, we ask God to "forgive us our trespasses as we forgive those who trespass against us." Jesus goes on to say that if we forgive others their transgressions, then our heavenly Father will forgive us ours, but if we fail to forgive others, we will not receive God's forgiveness. So you're correct, Richard, in saying that we have to hold up our end of the bargain, as it were. Jesus underscores the importance of the virtue of forgiveness in an exchange with Peter. The apostle asks Jesus how often would he have to forgive a brother who had sinned against him. "As many as seven times?" Peter asks. Jesus's response is "… not seven times, but seventy-seven times." Countless times, really. If we want divine mercy, we must extend forgiveness to our brothers and sisters. Doing so may run counter to our wounded feelings and our human instincts, but the imperative is clear: we must be able to feel true forgiveness for others in order to warrant God's mercy and forgiveness for ourselves. And the ultimate source of that virtue of forgiveness is love, which we are commanded to have not only for God but for all our fellow human beings as well.

To forgive and forget. We are clearly enjoined to forgive others in the Our Father, but the prayer doesn't mention *forgetting* what it was that offended or wounded us. I would like to share a personal experience with the need for forgiveness—one that goes back almost fifty years but that I've never forgotten. My younger brother Anthony, who was born with a heart defect, was playing with a neighborhood friend. The boys were both eight years old; I was sixteen at the time. The scene was our yard, and I happened to walk outside when the young neighbor suddenly became angry at Anthony—I seem to recall it was over Anthony's not wanting to play a game he had suggested. By way of background, I should add that this incident occurred a few weeks before my brother was scheduled for his third heart surgery, an operation that, though risky, we hoped would give him the chance to lead a normal life. I remember the words my brother's friend shouted at him, as hurtful and cruel as anything he could have said. "Anthony," he screamed, "when you go to the hospital for your operation, I hope you die!" I'm sure that little boy didn't really mean what he said that day, but the words proved prophetic. Anthony's surgery was successful, but he subsequently developed pneumonia and other complications. He passed away on July 23, 1965, about a month after his friend had screamed that malediction at him. Was I angry at the boy? Most certainly, and deeply so. I was also enraged at God for doing nothing to help my brother, for not answering my prayers. How, then, could I help feeling antipathy and bitterness toward the young boy who had wished my brother dead and had been granted his request?

Anthony's death sent shock waves through my large family. In some ways, we still bear the scars of that cataclysmic event. Personally, I harbored deep resentment toward his young friend for some time. I never confronted him with the cruel words he had spewed at Anthony that day, but I often wondered if he, in the inner recesses of his heart, ever asked my brother for forgiveness. I know Anthony would have granted it; he was a peaceful, loving boy to whom arguments were unknown territory.

Thankfully, the passage of time and the ability to view the incident from the perspective of adulthood have allowed me to forgive my brother's friend without reservation. But it's certainly evident that I've never forgotten what happened that day. Perhaps that's God's plan. My remembrance of the unthinking words of a young boy to his friend so long ago has served a useful purpose: it has, at times, helped prevent me from using my own ill-considered words to hurt someone else. Forgiving and remembering, in this case, have made more sense than forgiving and forgetting.

RC Yes, you are correct, Jerry. In this case, "forgiving and remembering" made more sense to you than letting that deeply disturbing incident slip from your memory. But all of us must take into account your words: "...the passage of time and the ability to view the incident from the perspective of adulthood…." Many people, despite maturing physically, find that their remembrance of a subject does not help them mitigate the pain that subject still brings them. In fact, what happens with many painful memories is that they become crystallized, and when they are touched upon they bring anguish instead of insight.

Since I have known you, I have listened quietly to your pain about the loss of your beloved sibling, Anthony. The story always struck me as remarkable because of the number of siblings present in the Pitarresi home—I believe there were ten, including Anthony. I thought it was remarkable that you continued to mourn his loss, despite the blessing of such a large family. But as I have aged, and as I watch over my now aged mother, ninety-three and counting, I have learned that the pain of a loss cannot be relativized. Anthony is mourned because he will always be a part of your family. His remembrance, then, not only makes more sense for your family; it is part of a religious principle. Judaism elevated the concept of *remembrance* to the level of a commandment: "Remember the Sabbath day and keep it holy" (Exod. 20:8). "Remember what Amalek did to you on your journey out of Egypt" (Deut.25:17). At special holiday seasons during the Jewish calendar year, we have a service of *Yizkor,* a memorial for those whom we have loved and lost in the recent and distant past. *Yizkor* comes from the word "remember." When you think of Anthony and pray for his soul in the world of eternity, you are preserving the blessing of his memory for you and your family. Likewise, your sons, although you worry about their religious connection to the ancestral faith, will preserve Anthony's remembrance through their generations. Immortality is a difficult subject, but I believe memory comprises the greatest part of understanding what it means.

At the end of every prayer service in Jewish life, we recite the *Kaddish.* That word is derived from the Hebrew word for "holiness." It is referred to as the Mourner's Prayer. Interestingly, there is no mention of the deceased in its recitation. It is a doxology—a prayer of praising God's works. Yet the Reform movement in Judaism added a paragraph taken from the *Kaddish D'Rabbanan*—the Memorial Prayer for the rabbis of old. This prayer mentions the deceased and the need to preserve the memories of all our loved ones. It reads:

> The departed whom we now remember have entered into the peace of life eternal. They still live on earth in the acts of goodness they performed and in the hearts of those who cherish their memory. May the beauty of their life abide among us as a loving benediction. May the Father of peace send peace to all who mourn, and comfort all the bereaved among us.
>
> Amen

How lucky you were to have shared in the exquisitely beautiful eight years of Anthony's existence. How wise and perceptive you are to preserve his memory through your loving prayers throughout the years. May Anthony's memory continue to heal your aching heart and shower upon all of you the blessings of comfort, joy, and peace.

Allow me to share yet another perspective on forgiving and forgetting. One of the great authors of the Holocaust period, Primo Levi, talked about the difficulty of memory. He submitted that a memory we keep coming back to, or that keeps popping up in our thoughts and dreams years after the fact, has most likely crystallized. As a result, the memory of what actually occurred has transformed and become something else, even something inaccurate or false.

Recently, I shared lunch with a thoughtful, talented, dear friend whom I had hired way back in the 1980s to help me teach Hebrew at the Dalton School in New York. Two and a half hours later, Jerry, I had what we call a *chiddush,* an insight into a memory that has pursued and afflicted me over the years.

Fran had married within the last decade, as had I. (That she married a guy named Richard who was born in Buffalo should amuse you, an inveterate Western New Yorker!) She was surprised and delighted to hear that Jeanne and I had recited marital vows four years before. And we spoke about what had delayed my remarriage, as well as what had finally enabled her to marry her beloved Richard after so many years of "singlehood."

And here it was. Fran said, "I was finally able to meet and marry my husband when I gave up the fantasy of what I wanted and needed in a relationship."

Jerry, I was rendered speechless, which isn't an easy feat.

What the two of us have shared since we first became friends at Hamilton is a love of the aesthetic. Academically and intellectually, that drew us to the classics in literature and in the art world. Physically, that inspired us to pursue the Greek ideal of a well-formed body and limbs (you came a lot closer than I in those days to achieving a semblance of Michelangelo's *David*). As a reflection of our love of beauty, we were naturally drawn to beautiful women.

Returning to "singledom" after a score of years with Debbie, I had the opportunity to activate this latter inclination. In other words, I dated the most physically attractive people I could meet. The results were often disastrous and inevitably caused me great regret.

Fran's words punctured my thinking, thank God. Perhaps I was coming to that conclusion anyway, and she just said the right thing at the right time. I can make a lot of excuses about this vain, superficial pursuit all these years (my mother was the original family aesthete), but I take responsibility for my own inability to surmount this affliction. This is not to say that I do not appreciate physical beauty. I find my wife, Jeanne, very beautiful. But when beauty becomes the principal subject rather than its complement, there is a severe problem.

And this goes back to our discussion about temptation. If we do not recognize our tendencies to head in the wrong direction, we can wind up in places we really don't want to be (although we are often hell-bent on getting there). I am slow to forgive myself for certain behaviors, as you know. But I know for certain that I don't want to forget this behavioral pattern, because it has disturbed me, even plagued me, for many years now.

I am grateful for Fran's words. At this point, not forgiving and not forgetting may be the best course to follow.

JP Richard, it seems to me that your lunch conversation with your friend Fran, and the insight you gained from it, were preordained. Your attraction to beauty in its various manifestations—art, literature, and the human form—is understandable. As you mentioned, I share that trait with you (and we are certainly not alone). We've both seen Michelangelo's *David* in the *Galleria dell Accademia* in Florence; the exquisiteness of that masterpiece literally takes one's breath away. We often discuss books we've read, sharing the gracefulness of a particular writer's style. And, as you said, we both appreciate feminine beauty. I see nothing untoward in that—to a point.

As you make clear, the ideal of beauty can become our focus, blinding us, in your words, to the "substance behind the beauty" (or in some cases, the lack of substance). The worth of others is measured by their physical attractiveness or abilities, a specious but all too common way of valuing people in our world today. It occurs to me that this predilection is another of the temptations we face as human beings. Jesus's tempting by Satan in the desert didn't include a bevy of beautiful sirens luring him to pay homage to the Prince of Darkness, but I can understand why it might have. As Catholics, we believe Jesus had both divine and human natures. Despite his sharing our humanity, I'm sure Jesus still wouldn't have succumbed to the devil's machinations. With beauty, the danger for us lies in becoming enthralled by it and forgetting its ultimate source, which is God, of course. His purpose in creating the beauty of the human form was not, I'm rather certain, so we could walk around with a lovely trophy on our arm. Other people aren't created to satisfy our needs—that's what "things" are for. When we see all people as having worth, in and of themselves and regardless of their appearance and their station in life, then we're closer to what Jesus preached. That's worth remembering, I think, in a world that prizes beauty, athleticism, and youthfulness as much as ours does.

As for you, Richard, you have done well not to forget your flirtation with beauty for beauty's sake, but it's time you forgave yourself. You shed that behavior long ago, and you have found, in the beautiful marriage you share with Jeanne, the substance that was lacking in other relationships you experienced.

THE GRACE OF GOD

JP I'm sure you heard the expression, "There, but for the grace of God, go I." I wasn't sure who is credited with first uttering these familiar words, or just what the person meant by them, so I researched the quotation. The statement has been attributed to John Bradford, an Englishman who lived in the mid-sixteenth century. Bradford supposedly made the observation when he witnessed condemned men being led to the gallows. An added twist to the story is that Bradford himself was ultimately burned at the stake for his religious beliefs (he was a staunch Protestant during the reign of Mary, Queen of Scots), which makes me wonder if anyone witnessing his horrible death had the same thought Bradford has been credited with, rightly or wrongly.

What does the quotation mean, Richard? I think that depends on who is interpreting it. Some people see it as a way of connecting sympathetically with the misfortunes of others, of feeling compassion for those who have been slighted or treated unfairly by life through no fault of their own. As a Catholic, I see the statement as an invitation to empathize with the suffering of others and an acknowledgment that our lives—our ultimate fates—are dependent on someone and something beyond ourselves, namely God and the gift of his grace. It's an expression of humility, an admission that, despite what we may think, we aren't in full control of our lives. The quotation could serve as the antidote for the most destructive of the Seven Deadly Sins, the sin of pride. When we see others who are struggling with difficult circumstances, we sense that we have been "graced" by God through not having to experience the same plight. While pride can lead us to deny God's preeminent role in our lives or to attempt to put ourselves on an equal footing with God (we need only refer to our first parents in the book of Genesis), humility allows us to recognize and acknowledge our dependence on God.

Interestingly, I found that some people see the statement as a prideful one. Doing so, I think, requires interpreting the words as divisive rather than building bridges between people. This reading of "there but for the grace of God go I" suggests that the speaker has an inflated sense of self-worth that puts him or her above another less-fortunate human being. Jesus's parable of the Pharisee and the Publican in the Gospel of St. Luke (18:9–14) comes to mind. Both men went to the temple to pray. The Pharisee sanctimoniously thanked God that he wasn't like other men who were sinners, naming among them the Publican, a tax collector, who felt unworthy and stood in the back of the temple. The Publican, for his part, acknowledged that he was a sinner, beat his breast, and asked for God's mercy. Jesus concludes the parable by saying that only the Publican went forth from the temple justified. Jesus's message is about the need for humility and the harmful effects of pride. In that sense, the statement could be read as a cautionary one rather than an admission of one's dependence on God's grace.

As I mentioned above, I see the quotation as one that helps me to empathize with the sufferings of others as well as to give thanks for the blessings I have been graced with by God. I truly believe that all that I am and all that I have are gifts from God. While I won't presume to know the mind of God, my sense is that the grace from which I benefit was given to move me to reach out to others rather than to separate me from them.

RC To understand our life as a gift of God is central to all theological thought. Yet the "grace" God bestows upon us—that needs special attention. The word in Hebrew is *chen,* which can be translated as "grace," "beauty," "charm," "favor," and "loveliness." There is a passage from the book of Proverbs, known as the "Woman of Valor," that is traditionally recited by a husband to his wife during the Friday night celebration of the Sabbath. It ends with these verses: "Charm (*chen*) is deceitful, and beauty is vain, but a woman who fears the Lord is to be praised. Give her a share in the fruit of her hands, and let her works praise her in the city gates" (Prov. 31:30–31).

Chen is seen pejoratively here—translated as "charm" or even better, perhaps, as "attractiveness." In other words, we're speaking of something superficial—a lower understanding of the aesthetic, if you will. Perhaps, in this case, we're speaking of the appeal of an outer beauty, one that Judaism recognizes in all descriptions of our biblical matriarchs. Yes, our scriptural heroines were physically beautiful, but if the beauty were only exterior, our understanding of grace would be hollow.

We move, then, to the idea that all grace is a gift of God, exterior and interior. We could posit then that all gifts—intellectual, physical (athletic), spiritual—are divinely endowed. During the High Holy Days, standing before the Holy Ark, about to lift the Torah, God's greatest gift, we recite the Thirteen Attributes of God. In the Bible, these verses punctuate a perilous time in Israelite history. The people have sinned against the Almighty through the building of the Golden Calf. Moses pleads for mercy on behalf of his sinning congregation, and God is merciful, renewing the Covenant with his people once again. The Lord proclaims: "The Lord, the Lord, a God merciful and **gracious,** slow to anger, and abounding in steadfast love and faithfulness, keeping steadfast love for thousands, forgiving iniquity and transgression and sin..." (Exod. 34:6–7). The adjective *gracious (chanun)* suggests in this context a divinity who cares for his human creation.

I think we both agree that it is our obligation to serve the world *imitatio dei*. We are given, through Moses, an insight into divine attributes. We must emulate God by being merciful, gracious, compassionate, slow to anger, *et alia*—at least in our own frail human way. It is this last understanding of grace (*chen*) that dovetails with your own belief that God graces us with His presence, and through that grace endows us with the gifts to help our loved ones and others less fortunate than ourselves.

But there is more to glean from our idea of God's grace. The Greek equivalent of *chen* is *xaris.* From *xaris* we derive the English word *charisma.* One does not learn or acquire charisma; it is a gift from God. We tend to think of the term *charismatic* when we think of TV personalities and politicians. Yet the word was originally attributed to Christians who could heal others through the gift of the Holy Spirit.

We return to our saying—"There, but for the grace of God, go I." Receiving God's grace, as we see, is a complex mission. Rich or poor, successful or failing, able or disabled, we are all recipients of God's grace. Certainly it is not true that all our gifts are equally endowed, but it is incumbent upon those of us who are blessed with an abundance of *chen* to be generous with those who both need and ask for our help.

JP Great reflection—scholarly but still very accessible, I believe. To add to the discussion, the word *charism,* as used in Catholic theology, means a gift of the Holy Spirit (seven specific ones are identified) given to a person so that he or she can employ it in some useful way to add to the life of the Church. And the mission of the Church is to bring all people into a relationship with God, to experience and know God's love. You probably already know that the seven gifts are found in Isaiah 11:2–3. Here is a brief description of them from the Catholic perspective, taken from the Catechism of the Catholic Church:

The seven gifts of the Holy Spirit are wisdom, understanding, counsel, fortitude, knowledge, piety, and fear of the Lord. They belong in their fullness to Christ, Son of David. They complete and perfect the virtues of those who receive them. They make the faithful docile in readily obeying divine inspirations.

The gifts of the Holy Spirit fully embodied in Jesus Christ, abound as well in all Christians who are in a state of grace. We receive them when we are filled with sanctifying grace, the life of God within us—as, for example, when we receive a sacrament, such as the Eucharist, worthily. Infused with these gifts, we respond to the promptings of the Holy Spirit as if by instinct, the way Christ himself would.

RC First, Brother Jerry, may I confess that I was not aware of six of these "Gifts of the Spirit" as they appear in Catholicism. The seventh gift, piety, comes from the Greek translation of the Bible, the Septuagint. But I am deeply touched by the words: "We receive them (these gifts) when we are infused with sanctifying grace…as, for example, when we receive a sacrament, such as the Eucharist, worthily." I have been dwelling for some time now on this sentence. How do we "receive a sacrament worthily?" Do we receive these gifts as a reward for offering up our prayers to God in true and sincere devotion? Do we not have to display at the beginning, even before we receive infusion of God's Spirit, some form of those heavenly gifts you have described? For example, if we do not pray with piety, how can God reward us with the gift of piety? Or is it a higher level of piety that he bestows upon the pious believer?

Church- and synagogue-goers, at all times, come looking for answers to their questions. We'd all love to be recipients of these gifts, but how can the person who enters the church or synagogue acquire them? It seems that much work, including much reading and study, is a prerequisite for this acquisition. Even then, if we are blessed to receive the gifts, we know that we do not always use them properly.

In the Mishnaic tractate known as "Sayings of the Fathers," it says: "Turn over the Torah, and turn it again, for every thing is in it; contemplate it, and grow gray and old over it; for thou canst have no better rule than this." Employing your seven gifts, I would submit the following: study, in Judaism, leads to knowledge; knowledge leads to wisdom; wisdom leads to understanding; understanding leads to counsel; it is all buttressed by prayer, which leads to piety; piety leads to fear of the Lord; fear of the Lord leads to fortitude. I took the liberty of prefacing these gifts with the gift of study, of paramount importance in Jewish life.

TAKING CARE OF THE ELDERLY

You shall rise up before the aged, and defer to the old, and you shall fear your God (Lev. 19:32).

RC Yesterday I read a piece in the *New York Times* by a Chinese author named Yu Hua, in which he discusses a revised Chinese law regarding the protection of the rights and interests of elderly people. A new clause asserts: "Family members living apart from the elderly should frequently visit or send greetings to the elderly persons." To which I would respond, employing the modern idiom: "Really?" Do we really need to legislate concern for our parents and grandparents? Wasn't that pretty well taken care of by the fourth commandment: "Thou shalt honor thy Father and thy Mother"? What has happened to the ABCs of moral behavior, dear friend? We explicitly knew what was right or wrong growing up. There wasn't an option when it came to caring for the elderly. My mother's mother came to live with us when her husband died. My father, of blessed memory, was a devoted son to his parents. I know how often you drove to Niagara Falls to visit your aging parents over the years and how deeply you believe in the explicit religious obligation to care for those who nurtured us in our early years. Has the loss of physical proximity to our families (Avery Korman's book, The *Old Neighborhood,* illustrates this well) led to a loss of connection to our nearest kinfolk? I'm not sure, but I know this is a topic close to your heart.

JP It truly is a topic I care about very much, Richard. I was fortunate to grow up in a large extended family in Niagara Falls, and my parents instilled in my brothers and sisters and me the importance of respecting and honoring my grandparents as well as our numerous aunts and uncles. The commandment "Honor thy Father and thy Mother" extended to all the older relatives we saw on a regular basis growing up. As I grew up and eventually went away to college, ultimately resettling some two hundred miles away from my family, that dictum still informed my life. I made those trips home to offer my parents help with whatever they might need and to maintain my connection with my grandparents. My mother used to remind me to visit them, as well as my aunts and uncles, but she really didn't have to do so—a trip home didn't feel complete unless I saw them. I guess I had internalized the fourth commandment by that point in my life. Sadly, I have only one aunt on my father's side left, and one aunt and uncle on my mother's side, but I stay in close contact with them. It just feels like the right thing to do for me—maybe that's why the commandment was carved on those tablets that Moses brought down from Mt. Sinai.

RC So what's happened? Have we failed to instill in our children the lessons we learned at home, in church, and in synagogue? It seems to me that there is a basic, primordial need to care for those who cared for us when we were growing up. How can we ignore the needs of those who gave much of their lives so that we could become healthy adults? It seems we diminish who we are by forgetting our elderly.

JP The elderly can be marginalized, I'm afraid, if we don't make the effort to make them part of our lives. Each year at the holidays, I take the students in the religious education class I teach to one of our nursing homes to decorate. For some kids, it's the first time they've been to such a facility. Many of them don't have grandparents or other elderly relatives in our area, so it's an opportunity to interact with people they normally don't see or even think about too often. When I ask them later to give feedback about their experience at the nursing home, they are invariably positive about the visit. In terms of Catholic theology, they are practicing one of the corporal works of mercy in visiting the sick and infirm. I try to make the kids understand that this is what we are called upon to do as a faith community.

RC In Judaism, *bikkur cholim*, "visiting the sick," is seen as the highest form of behavior. So, clearly, the imperative to care for others is a preeminent principle of both our faiths. But I wonder if all the children who participate in this visit to the nursing homes (I've done the same with the young people in our religious school) feel a need to become closer to their own grandparents, who become infirm as they approach their mortality. I guess it really depends upon us, the parents. Perhaps we're failing to implant in our children the seeds that were implanted within us. We seem to have been successful with our children, in both our families, but that is obviously the exception rather than the rule in society.

JP I know that my bond with my grandparents was nurtured and strengthened first through Sunday dinners at their home—their flat, actually, on the second floor of the three-story dwelling that housed them and two other families of my relatives. When our extended family grew too large to fit in my grandparents' house, our Sunday ritual changed—Grandma and Grandpa made visits to each of their children's families. Those visits from the matriarch and patriarch of our family (on my mother's side) were a highlight of our Sundays growing up. And perhaps without being aware of it, my siblings and I were learning lessons about the importance of family and the inter-generational connectedness that forms its bedrock. That paradigm has become much less common today, to be sure, and I don't think we're better for it.

RC Yes, I agree…sadly though. Isn't it interesting, Jerry, that it seems to be part of human nature to think that things get better with each succeeding generation? But—and this is not nostalgic—we've lost something very precious with this paradigm shift in family life. Jeanne's memories of her childhood—beginning with church on Sunday, followed by Sunday afternoon lunch with parents and grandparents—are very similar to your youthful remembrance.

So are we going to fall flat here? If we don't have our elders in our midst, what can we do about maintaining our love and concern for them? First, more effort in maintaining those relationships is required, as well as more face-to-face meetings. If we continue to make the effort, our children will recognize how much we value the connection between generations. "Thou shalt teach them to thy children...." So goes our prayer we call the *V'ahavta*. Teaching children is a full-time occupation, and it involves every generation of our people. If our children do not acquire the wisdom of their elders, they will be sorely lacking in the historical narrative of their family. Break the chain of our generations and we break the bonds that tie us together—familial, social, and religious. It's a dangerous course. The answer is patent: we must take steps to ensure our families' health and survival.

JP I wholeheartedly agree—it's vitally important for all of us to maintain the connections between generations, along with the valuable life lessons they provide us and our children.

THE AFTERLIFE: A JEWISH VIEW

This world is an antechamber for the world to come; prepare yourself in the antechamber so that you may enter the banquet hall (Sayings of the Fathers 4:21).

JP Recently, I read a column by Rabbi Marc Gellman in which a reader posed the question of whether Judaism maintained a belief in the afterlife. The short answer was yes, but I have a feeling there's more to the subject to be explored.

RC This is a great topic to consider, and one many Jews ignore because they believe that there is no concept of heaven or hell in Judaism. You've heard it many times: the Jews believe that it's all about *this world*, while Christians believe it's about *the world to come.* I will tell you with some embarrassment that it was not until I began studying the rabbinic literature that I came across the idea of what we call in Hebrew the *olam habo,* literally the "coming world." Let's explore what that means.

We'll begin with the blissful idea, held by many, many people, that we will see our departed loved ones at the end of our earthly career. This is certainly a prayer most of us would love to see answered, but it is something we'll never be able to know until we experience our own mortality. The rabbis of late antiquity believed that the "next world" would parallel "this world" in an ideal way. That is, as they studied the Bible and rabbinic literature in the academies and prayed in the synagogue every day, so too would they continue the same practices in heaven, reunited with all their revered teachers and, by extension, their loved ones. No eternal relaxation for them, nor heavenly tee-off times. Study and reverence for God were the hallowed desiderata of the next world, as they were on earth.

But now let's return to the difficult subject of how the Jewish view of the afterlife evolved theologically. *Nowhere* in the pages of the Bible are there specific references to heaven or hell. We Jews, before we "ran into" the Persians and Greeks, were a remarkably *un*-philosophical people. But after contact with the Zoroastrian teachings and the influence of Hellenistic writings, we began seeing more than what was in front of us. That is, the Garden of Eden, a specific place in the book of Genesis, was translated into the Greek Septuagint as *paradise.* According to this perspective, the original geographic locale now was seen as a "place" where righteous souls would go as a just reward for their labors on earth.

And as for the concept of hell, well, life is a series of opposites, is it not? If the righteous had a paradise, certainly the evildoers had another place, That place, *Gehinnom*, was a real locale south of Jerusalem, where in ancient times children were sacrificed to the God Moloch (cf., Josh. 15:8; 2 Kings 23:10). *Gehinnom*, the place, gradually transformed into the Hebraic *gehenna,* an expression for anything that was evil or sinful. Hell, which is derived from the Old Norse goddess of the underworld, Hel, eventually became synonymous with *gehenna.*

So by the time of the Talmud, we read about one of our greatest scholars, Rabbi Johanan ben Zakkai, pondering what will happen to him when he dies. He weeps before his students, who are incredulous and want to know the source of his misery. Rabbi Johanan responds:

> Now that I am being taken before the supreme King of Kings, who lives and endures for ever and ever, whose anger, if He is angry with me, is an everlasting anger, who if He imprisons me imprisons me for ever, who if He puts me to death puts me to death for ever, and whom I cannot persuade with words or bribe with money—nay more, when there are two ways before me, one leading to Paradise (*Gan Eden,* in Hebrew) and the other to Hell (*Gehinnom*), and I do not know by which I shall be taken, shall I not weep?" (Berachot 28b).

How can the change in *our* thinking be more explicit than this sympathetic rendering of a righteous man wondering about his destiny in the world to come? But…Judaism continues to change over the centuries. Paradise, the Garden of Eden, by the time of the thirteenth-century medieval commentator Nachmanides, becomes a repository not for our physical bodies but for our souls! Maimonides, undoubtedly our greatest scholar and sage, had written a century earlier, "There are neither bodies nor bodily forms in the world-to come, only the souls of the righteous" (Mishneh Torah, Hilchot Teshuvah 8).

And let's get personal here. I was brought up in a family that was guided by the philosophical principles of Reform Judaism. My concept of the "next world" was derived from the Union Prayer Book, and I note particularly the following English words that accompany the *Kaddish*, our Mourners Prayer. On page 152 of the UPB we read:

> The departed whom we now remember have entered into the peace of life eternal. They still live on earth in the acts of goodness they performed and in the hearts of those who cherish their memory. May the beauty of their life abide among us as a loving benediction. May the Father of peace send peace to all who mourn, and comfort all the bereaved among us.

The paragraph supports a very precious Jewish idea: that while we may never be able to confirm what happens after our loved ones die—whither they go and whether we will ever see them again—their sustained presence ("they still live on earth") in our lives is a result of our remembrance of who and what they represented to us, their grateful offspring. *Remembrance* is not an option in Jewish life. "Remember the Sabbath day and keep it holy" (Exod. 20:8); "Remember what Amalek did to you on your journey out of Egypt" (Deut. 25:17). It is our remembrance, and our recollection of that remembrance to each succeeding generation, that affirms our faith in all our ancestors—from Abraham and Sarah, our founding father and mother, to Mom and Dad, who continue to accompany us on all our journeys. In a sense then, the concept of immortality is in our hearts and in our souls, forging an inextricable bond between this world and the next.

The Afterlife—A Christian Perspective

JP The Mourners Prayer from the Union Prayer Book is both beautiful and comforting. To remember our loved ones, the good lives they led, and the values they passed on to us is a link that connects our present world and the one to come. And Christianity (and Catholicism) makes clear that we are destined for something beyond our earthly existence.

The existence of heaven and hell has been discussed and debated throughout human history. Do we live on in some way after our earthly life is over? Is there a heaven—and its counterpart, a hell? If there is an afterlife, what is it like? Do people get rewarded for living a "good" life? Conversely, do other people get punished for living a "bad" life? These are age-old questions, to be sure.

Christianity and Catholicism are unequivocal on the subject of an afterlife. I've attended many funeral Masses over the years, and while the sadness of the bereaved is palpable, the liturgy makes clear the belief that the physical death of the loved one is actually a rebirth into a new life. That new life, whatever form it takes, is one united with God in his heavenly kingdom, described in various images as the "new Jerusalem," a dwelling place with many rooms, or an eternal wedding banquet. And as support for that spiritual rebirth, Christians have the death and resurrection of Jesus Christ, truly the *sine qua non* upon which Christianity rises and falls.

St. Paul makes this clear in his first epistle to the Corinthians, chapter fifteen. If there is no resurrection of the dead, then Christ has not risen. It follows that if Christ did not rise from the dead, his horribly painful death on the cross had no meaning or import for humanity. Thus, we who believe Christ died in expiation for our sins and to open the gates of heaven for our own rebirth have no hope of an eternal afterlife in union with God the Father, Jesus, and the Holy Spirit. But Paul argues that death is *not* the final answer: "Death, where is thy victory? Death, where is thy sting?" (I Cor. 15:55). Paul almost taunts death in his personification of it because he is so thoroughly convinced of Jesus's resurrection, which he argues foreshadows and promises our own. Like many converts, Paul is zealous in his beliefs and his desire to have others share them, but he definitely zeroes in on the very heart of Christian belief: Jesus's sacrificial death and glorious resurrection. Judaism, as you observed, places great emphasis on remembrance and recollection of watershed events and personages in its history; for Christians, the resurrection of Jesus is *the* watershed event on which all else depends. If Jesus did not rise from the dead, then we have no hope of doing the same.

Just what is heaven like? The Catechism of the Catholic Church defines it as "the ultimate end and fulfillment of the deepest human longings, the state of supreme definitive happiness." Despite people who have recounted their near-death experiences, speaking of seeing a brilliant white light, and books such as *Heaven Is for Real,* which describe the heavenly realm in various ways, no one knows. Catholics believe we will experience a "beatific vision" when we are reborn into eternal life. That vision involves contemplation of God in all his heavenly glory, something we can only get a brief glimpse of in our corporeal, temporal lives. Absolute love, transcendent love, beyond anything we can know on earth is what that experience would afford us—for eternity, of course. Worth dying for, most people would agree.

On the subject of the afterlife, I read that the Hindus believe the soul, rather than *being* absorbed by the absolute source of all goodness and love and thus reduced to nothingness, instead absorbs that source into itself and retains its individuality in a heightened state. I like that concept, especially because I believe that God has made each of us a unique, individual creation and loves us as such.

Catholicism also teaches that our bodies will, in some way, take part in our resurrection; we will not be spirits moving like wind through the boughs of a tree. The Apostles Creed, which sometimes takes the place of the Nicene Creed as the profession of faith at Mass, states that we as Catholics believe in the communion of saints—that is, all souls in heaven—as well as "the resurrection of the body." That resurrected body will be a glorified one, able to do what Jesus did in His post-resurrection appearances, such as pass through walls and appear suddenly out of thin air, as it were. Who needs the magic of David Copperfield in the afterlife?

The alternative to heaven is, of course, something most people prefer not to think about, but Christianity is clear that hell exists. The Nicene and Apostles Creeds both contain direct references to Judgment Day and to Jesus as the just judge who will reward and condemn people according to their deserts. Dante's *Inferno* is the source of the stereotypical fiery hell populated by demons exacting horrible punishment on the hapless souls whom Jesus has condemned to perdition. But Catholic teaching really takes a different view, one that I ascribe to. The Catechism of the Catholic Church defines hell as "*eternal* separation from God, the source of all goodness and love and happiness for which human beings were created." What could be worse? Having free will, we make the choice to follow the path of righteousness that will ultimately lead us to union with God in heaven, or to turn away from God and walk down a dark road. No one is predestined to spend eternity in hell. We choose to alienate ourselves from the source of absolute love and goodness.

In essence, it's Hawthorne's unpardonable sin taken to the most extreme degree. God loves all of his creation, and he desires deeply that all people be saved. This God, who created human beings out of ineffable love, reminds me of the God described by Rabbi Harold Kushner, the author of *When Bad Things Happen to Good People*. In Rabbi Kushner's understanding, God mourns with us because of the misfortunes and tragedies that befall us through no fault of our own, and he mourns for us because of our own willful choice to reject him and the love he offers us. But he permits us to make that choice, always ready to receive us with open arms and extend his mercy to us if we awaken to the folly of our ways and seek to follow him and his commandments (as we see clearly in Jesus's parable of the Prodigal Son).

The key point about the afterlife, whether it be heavenly or hellish, is that it is for *eternity*. That's a concept that the human mind simply cannot comprehend. For the Christian, the stakes are indeed high, the paths are clear, and the choice is one each person has to make on his or her own. No one who professes a belief in Jesus Christ and his teachings can't say he or she wasn't aware.

I purposely didn't address the concept of purgatory here. The Catholic Church still believes in the existence of such a "way station" to heaven, but I remain conflicted about it. When I think of my parents, my younger brother, and other loved ones, I can't see why they wouldn't have been on the express train to heaven. The belief in limbo, the abode of the unbaptized, especially children, thankfully has fallen away.

FLEXIBILITY

Stay committed to your decisions, but stay flexible in your approach.

—Anthony Robbins, Life Coach

RC Well, Jerry, as Joe Nuxhall used to say at the end of the Cincinnati Reds radio broadcast, "Here's the old lefthander, rounding third and heading for home." I always liked that, dear friend. And I think it's time for us to do the same, although at this age I'm not trying a headfirst slide!

At any rate, I'd just like to touch on the topic of flexibility before we end these two-way epistles. You know everyone today talks about weight control, yoga, pilates, water aerobics, and other forms of keeping oneself in shape, but the most important aspect of that is flexibility. Flexibility is a deterrent to injury, and it helps ward off the effects of aging.

At the same time, while engaging in exercise that increases my flexibility (particularly swimming), I have become increasingly aware of my mortality. This I attribute to my father who, while living, taught me many lessons about the Jewish form of communal mourning. He taught me many more lessons as he faced, years ago, his own mortality.

In a tangential way, each morning I read at least one or two obituaries reported in the *New York Times.* Why? They fascinate me. I learn about people's contributions to the world, about the times in which they lived, and about the history they helped create. But most often I learn that the path to prominence is not a straight point from A to B. There are always more than a few zigs and zags along the way. The formula for success or renown is different for each person. Clearly, failure and disappointment enter every person's life. Yet what seems to be a common factor is each person's persistence in pursuing his or her goals no matter the set of circumstances he or she is presented with in life. Rich or poor, brilliant or average—those who succeed don't shirk from their life's vocations.

I think about the paths I have already traversed during these sixty-four years of living—the different locations, the different jobs, and the wonderful friends I have gathered on my journeys. To think that I would have remarried and acquired a stepdaughter, to think that I would have relocated to Florida before I was sixty, to think I would be working in Hot Springs, Arkansas, to think that I would be able to fulfill a dream to write a book with you via a self-publishing agency, well it wasn't "thinkable," and it wouldn't have happened if I was not open to new places, new possibilities in my life.

It's called life flexibility, which parallels physical "stretchability." Stretching myself through these recent years has been taxing, but every time I've stretched (or more accurately, been forced to stretch) the result has allowed me to become more flexible, more open about developments (good and bad) in my life.

I feel lucky to have arrived to this moment accompanied by a dear friend of old. As we continue to deepen ourselves in our faith traditions, let us continue to escort each other as we and our families wend our way along the path that leads to the future. *Ad majorem dei gloriam.*

JP Your thoughts about flexibility resonated with me, Richard. Like you, I too have learned the importance of maintaining flexibility; unfortunately, sometimes I've been taught those lessons through the pain of pulled muscles. As a person who likes to be physically active, I've been frustrated when a lack of flexibility has put me on the sidelines, as it were. But a regimen of rest and stretching has allowed me to get back into the race, to complete the metaphor.

Certainly, this physical stretching has its concomitant in what you've called "life flexibility." Each of our own personal odysseys has had its twists and turns. As the saying goes, life is what happens when you're busy making other plans. In contrast to you, I've spent my professional career in one job, in one place, but that doesn't mean I haven't experienced disappointments and challenges. At such times, I've learned to call upon my faith to sustain me. The prayer that I find particularly helpful in such times is the Our Father. In invoking it, we pray the words, "Thy will be done." That's really a recognition that, ultimately, our lives are in God's hands, even if we can't see that truth at a particular moment. Knowing that God is with us in the vicissitudes of life, that we are enveloped in his love, can give us the strength to deal with them, to stretch ourselves, and to become more open to what life brings our way.

The God that lies at the heart of each of our faith traditions has seen fit to provide us with a friendship that, for more than forty years, has transcended distance as well as personal trials and circumstances. For that I am most thankful. I echo your wish that we maintain that deep bond, continuing to grow as we walk along the path God in his wisdom has planned for us. And while we may be "rounding third and heading for home," in the words of Joe Nuxhall, my prayer is that we will enjoy many more years of friendship before people have the opportunity to read *our* respective obituaries. I'll leave that in God's hands.

29839746R00079

Made in the USA
Charleston, SC
25 May 2014